"Anne's book, *Saved,* is an honest account of the power of purpose and commitment, as an antidote to fear and loss. Anne walks through her deepest fears and discovers hope, humor and unconditional love amidst immense devastation. As she states 'Sanity dictates that you go with the flow, never knowing where it will take you.' Allow yourself to be inspired and to enjoy her wonderful journey!"

Annie Denver, MA
Aspen, CO

"If you look up the word hope in the dictionary you might just see Anne Gurchick's picture there. In the middle of her own battle with cancer she reaches out to save some of the most forgotten and battered victims of Hurricane Katrina. Anne's story is cause for celebration and the parallels between her journey to wellness and reaching out to the 'four leggeds' is further proof that we are inextricably connected to our animals and if we choose to listen, the lessons they give us can change our lives."

John St.Augustine
Radio Host and Author,
Every Moment Matters

"*Saved* is a celebration of friendship, in all of it various forms, that candidly brings to the forefront life's unexpected curve balls which can either destroy us or make us whole. Anne's irrepressible spirit proves that saving oneself is often easiest done by saving another, and her stories beg the reader to respect community on a universal level. This is a call to action: a reminder that the smallest gesture can make a world of difference, and finding beauty in what is broken is a special gift indeed."

Lisa Consiglio
Executive Director,
Aspen Writers' Foundation

"*Saved* reads like a conversation between Anne and a friend about her health issues while on a noble mission to rescue dogs after Hurricane Katrina. This is a significant memoir of a woman's personal journey, but more importantly, a view of the woman herself and an example of how we can make a difference."

Damiano de Sano Iocovozzi MSN FNP CNS
Author, *Don't Go to the Doctor without Me*

"*Saved* offers a side of the Hurricane Katrina disaster that was rarely reported or considered—the attempt to rescue and house thousands of family pets that were displaced from their owners. But the book is more than that: it is also a stirring memoir of a woman's effort to reclaim the vitality of her life through undertaking such a courageous act as rescue operations, halfway across the country. Saved! stirred my heart and reaffirmed the power of the and soul. It will stir yours, too."

—Robert Yehling
Author, *Writes of Life,*
Professor of Creative Writing,
Ananda College of Living Wisdom

Saved

A True Story

Cancer, Katrina Dogs and Me

ANNE GURCHICK

Transformation Media Books

Transformation Media Books

Published by Transformation Media Books, USA
www.TransformationMediaBooks.com

An imprint of Pen & Publish, Inc.
Bloomington, Indiana
(812) 837-9226
info@PenandPublish.com
www.PenandPublish.com

Cover photo, Anne and Stryder by Linda Koones

Cover photo, Stranded dogs in the Hurricane Katrina flooding
Copyright © 2005 Nanette Martin

Cover and text design by Jane Hagaman

ISBN: 978-0-9852737-2-9
Library of Congress Control Number: 2011943805

This book is printed on acid free paper.

Printed in the United States

Dedication

To
Melinda Goldrich, Bland Nesbit & Jan Panico
&
Hanuman, Hannah & Bella who were with me at the beginning
and comforted me throughout the journey

Acknowledgments

This book is the story of a short but significant period in my life, however, as with anyone, our life is not only about us but about the friends who accompany us on the journey. Friends who inspire us when we wane, provide confidence when we doubt, hope when we lose faith and humor when we need to smile. Our journey through life, while unique, is rarely a solo journey but more a team effort.

I don't know if I actually would have written this book if it weren't for Annie Denver who was the first to say "write it." My deepest gratitude to you for your friendship, for helping me find my way through some tough challenges and for providing a special retreat deep in the mountains where I could relax and refocus. Many thanks also to Jenny Deutschendorf who read the first few chapters and encouraged me to keep going. Our frequent hikes with our packs and long talks are always special.

Thanks also to Cheryl Wyly for being the first to read the story in its entirety, for loving it and giving me the confidence to actually agree to publish it when I wasn't sure I would.

Heartfelt thanks to my sister, Mary Louise Mayo, for dropping everything in her life and driving to Colorado to be with me during my long surgery and ensuing doctor appointments. She sat with me for hours as they prepared me for surgery and then continued to sit late into the night waiting for me to come out. She rarely thought about herself but only of keeping me comfortable.

To John St. Augustine for agreeing to look at a few pages, seeing a story and sending it to my publisher, Ginny Weissman. To Ginny for her guidance in writing, her comments and edits and, most importantly, for her shared passion and love for homeless animals and commitment to finding a place for them. To my publisher, Paul Burt, for his kindness, patience, contemplation and for making sure we got a great cover.

Many thanks, of course, to Bland Nesbit, who shares the same intense passion and love for homeless animals as I do. She is as dedicated as I am to ending the killing of as many innocent pets as we can. To Melinda Goldrich, a dear friend and so much a part of this story who, despite her abhorrence of any car trip over an hour, persevered through the long road trip home with humor and only brief moments of utter frustration. The memories of our trip are cherished and something we will both always look back on fondly. To Jan Panico for her friendship and positive attitude. Despite all the trying situations we found ourselves in, Jan remained calm and provided comfort and humor. Bland, Melinda and Jan's love for and desire to help animals made them the perfect accomplices on the adventure.

To Seth Sachson for opening the doors of animal rescue to me and for inviting me to be a part of what has become the most inspiring thing in my life, saving the lives of homeless animals about to be killed for no reason other than lack of space. As we worked together we became the best of friends and survived some trying times. Seth selflessly opened his heart and the Aspen Animal Shelter to allow us to bring in rescues that otherwise would have been killed. There aren't enough words of appreciation to express what that means and I am grateful to share his passion and learn from him. To the Aspen Animal Shelter staff, Chad Clark, Sadie Thimsen, Alex Lara and Victor Salas who selflessly work 24/7 providing shelter, love and socialization to so many homeless animals. These are the real heroes.

To my current pups Bella, Max, Stryder and Haddie who had to forego their daily hikes in order for me to finish this book but who did so willingly . . . most of the time. My love for you fills my heart and makes me smile.

Finally, to those who volunteered to help the animals displaced and left homeless by Hurricane Katrina and to animal rescue and welfare workers and volunteers everywhere. We face hardships and must make choices every day. It is devastating to each of us when an innocent animal must die and yet they do by the millions in our country every year. Keep up the fight—it is difficult and we have a long road and tough journey ahead of us but we are making a difference and *will* end the needless practice of killing adoptable pets in our country.

Adopt a shelter dog or cat—they are the most amazing pets and you are saving a life by doing so.

Bland, Jan, Liz, Anne and Melinda at their 2006 reunion

Chapter 1

"IT'S CANCER . . . AND IT'S BAD."

My eyes well with tears as Dr. Nelson speaks, his eyes bearing the compassion so necessary at a time like this. My gut wrenches and I can't breathe. The pain is unbearable but momentarily shadowed by panic. My safe and comfortable world has shattered into pieces that suspend in front of me, waiting for more information before they crash to the floor. I want to drop to the floor, right here in Dr. Nelson's office, close my eyes and curl up in a ball until what he has just said goes away.

I look at the big brown eyes staring back at me with concern. They belong to my sweet pea, Hannah, my gentle and loving Rottweiler. It isn't fair that her cancer has returned after such a valiant fight. Just six months ago, Dr. Nelson had assured me they had gotten it all and she would be fine. I thought we were clear on that.

He is speaking words that I can barely distinguish. His lips are moving; although I don't really hear him, somehow his words register. Hannah must start chemo tomorrow and I should take her to Colorado State University in Ft. Collins as soon as I reach Colorado.

I'm leaving Austin the day after tomorrow. My furniture and belongings are already gone. My mind is in turmoil trying to figure out how to pull everything together given this new development. It seems impossible.

I rush home and as I walk in my phone is ringing. My sister starts rattling details of her son's plan to arrive tomorrow to help me with my drive to Colorado. She's going on and on without pausing for a breath so I interrupt her.

"Hannah's cancer is back." Saying the words suddenly makes it all real. Painful emotions flood over me. This time, I throw myself down onto the couch, unable to deal as the grief hits me.

"I wish it was me and not her." I sob.

"Are you serious? Don't *ever* say anything like that again!" my sister reprimands. "Seriously—never again."

I wake early the next morning and rush Hannah to the veterinarian oncologist. By now she has stopped eating and will barely lift her head. It is heart wrenching. I love this little girl more than I ever thought possible. She will stay at the clinic overnight after receiving her first round of chemo and a battery of tests.

The next morning, I arrive for Hannah. Although her tests aren't back, she has been given the green light to travel, since her health has improved. Plus, we're heading to one of the best canine cancer centers in the country. The vet tech brings her out and I rush to hug her, burying my face in her familiar, sweet-smelling fur. She is equally excited to see me, and her little butt wiggles back and forth enthusiastically.

We hit the highway bright and early the following morning. Excited and anxious, I am on the cusp of fulfilling my dream of moving to the mountains. But a cloud of apprehension hangs over me as I think about the detour to the vet hospital in Ft. Collins and what it will bring. That afternoon, I'm lost in thought, speeding through the Texas panhandle, when my cell phone rings. I recognize the vet's number. I take a deep breath and answer, afraid of what she will tell me.

"Hi, Anne, this is Dr. Jenkins. I have Hannah's test results and I'm beyond confused. I really don't know what to say but the tests came back negative. There is no cancer."

I'm not sure I hear her correctly. "What? What do you mean? What does that mean?" I'm flabbergasted, flooded with mixed emotions.

"Again, I really don't know what to say. I'm happy they're negative, sorry Hannah went through the chemo and utterly baffled. I am glad you're heading to CSU as I'm eager to hear what they have to say."

We say our good-byes and all I can do is stare at the highway in front of me. Can I be so bold as to feel ecstatic? Could it be possible that the test results are correct? Would Hannah really be OK?

It was too good to be true.

When we got to the CSU vet hospital, Hannah was, indeed, cancer-free. They diagnosed her with a severe lung infection.

Just five months later, the words I cried out in anguish to my sister came back to haunt me. I was diagnosed with stage II breast cancer.

Chapter 2

I STARE IN THE MIRROR at my bald head, shallow skin and hollowed eyes. My head isn't bald, technically. It seems to be covered with a baby fine layer of what looks like peach fuzz. I finally have my eyebrows and eyelashes back. That makes me smile. It really does come down to the little things in life. It's been two months since I finished my chemotherapy and radiation treatments, and my body is a testament to the damage. I open my robe and look at the scars on my chest where my breasts used to be. I feel somewhat deformed, my once pert breasts replaced now with hard, round implants, my nipples replaced with scars that run the length of the implants. I run my finger over the scar just below my neck where the port that fed the chemo into my body had been located. I raise my right arm and look at the scars where the lymph nodes were removed. I pray that the cancer hasn't spread beyond the lymph nodes that tested positive.

This bodily inspection has become something of a routine for me. Finally past the shock of the diagnosis and the numbness of the months of treatment, I now find myself mesmerized, on a daily basis, with the aftermath. Having been poked, prodded, cut into, radiated and exposed to complete strangers, I still feel somewhat removed from my physical body. What I see in the mirror now isn't my body, but a roadmap of the cancer that tried to rob me of life. I refuse to let it. I think back to the day I was diagnosed, coming home and throwing myself on my bed. Alone. Scared. Lying in the fetal position and sobbing for what seemed like hours, but in reality was only ten or fifteen minutes. One day, life is normal and carefree, and the next, it's not. It's that quick. It's all so surreal, since I've never been sick other than the occasional flu or hangover. I let out a breath. *I'm alive,* I remind myself. *It could have been much worse.* I stand, looking at my naked body, trying to feel the depth of the experience but I'm unable to feel any emotion. Bored with staring at myself in the mirror, I search for a distraction to make me forget my bald head and scarred body.

In the background, I hear the television blasting the latest news about a hurricane in the Gulf of Mexico heading straight for New Orleans. I hear the name. I chuckle at the irony, thinking of my cousin's girlfriend, Katrina, who also has the ability to cause mass destruction, albeit emotional. The growing concern in the newscaster's voice again distracts me from my thoughts. Closing my robe, I turn to watch the coverage to see how close the hurricane actually is to landfall. A green-glow emanates from the television. As I walk closer, the picture captivates me. The radar image is of a hurricane that appears to be the size of the entire Gulf of Mexico and, yes, heading straight for New Orleans.

In the days that follow, I find myself glued to the television watching the twenty-four hour, live coverage of the mass evacuations along the Gulf Coast, followed by coverage of the storm as it slams ashore. I'm sure nothing could be worse than enduring this nightmare, but the devastating floods that follow prove me wrong. For the next two days, I watch in horror as thousands of people are left stranded on rooftops, begging to be rescued. I see the near-riots at the Superdome and the complete paralysis of the entire city's government. We all watch, a nation stunned at the surprising incompetence of our government and their inability to handle the disaster.

With mounting sadness, I watch people standing firm and refusing to leave their pets behind. My heart aches as they are forced to do so. Tears roll down their cheeks, distraught at being pulled off a rooftop and away from their beloved pet. Their confused and frightened pets stand abandoned in the flooded city. As coverage comes in from the streets, I realize these pets may be the lucky ones. Frightened and starving animals, once pampered family pets, fearfully roam the deserted streets. I am horrified when I hear stories of pets being left behind, chained to porches and drowning in the rising waters, unable to free themselves and swim to safety. Initially, I can't understand how anyone can leave their pets, given the enormity of the disaster. In the days that follow, I realize that the pets have been left for many reasons, but primarily because their owners had no choice. The pets aren't allowed into the shelters that have been set up. A person faced two choices: leave your pet, or potentially lose your life. Due to a lack of adequate disaster planning, these innocent animals are left to fight for their own survival and, in far too many cases, to die.

I look away from the television and stare out my window. It is a spectacular, clear, crisp early autumn day. The aspen trees high on the mountains are ablaze, a bright, sunshine yellow, contrasting against the dark green pines. The maple trees, sparsely scattered among the aspen and pine, have turned color, their leaves bright orange like glowing embers. I try to remind myself to look at the mountains every day. They make me forget, if only for a few minutes, my "cancer life." I love the mountains and feel privileged to live among their majestic beauty. It is a stark contrast to the scenes on the television, as I turn back to watch more of the Katrina coverage. Forgetting my own fears, I realize I want to be there, in New Orleans. I have to help care for these innocent animals and try to save as many of the beloved pets as possible.

Chapter 3

WE FIND A PRIVATE PLANE to get us there. Through a stroke of luck, a friend has connected with Katheryn, an animal shelter supporter. Not only does Katheryn have a plane, but she also really wants to travel with us and help the animals. She, too, has been watching the heartbreaking stories. Katheryn is passionate about animal welfare and will always generously give whatever she can in order to help animals in need. When she heard we were planning a trip, she immediately offered to take us on her plane.

Getting to Louisiana will not be a problem—or at least I hope not. In my search for sleeping accommodations, I again encounter the obvious. After a major hurricane, or any other natural disaster, hotel rooms are rare commodities. We'll be landing in Baytown, Texas, and will have to settle for a hotel in Beaumont, on the Texas/Louisiana state line, for the first night.

In my increasingly futile search for somewhere to stay while in Louisiana, I'm drawn into a phone conversation with a lady who has just told me she has no availability at her inn. As we chat about the hurricane's impact on her area, I tell her I'll be traveling from Colorado with a couple girlfriends to help care for the animals caught in the storm's aftermath.

"Oh, honey! That's so nice of y'all. Ya know, I might have someone who y'all can stay with. Let me check," she says, in her deep southern drawl. We hang up. Five minutes later, she calls back and says that yes, Liz, her son's ex-girlfriend, will let us stay in her lake house outside Baton Rouge. She gives me Liz LeJeune's telephone number and I thank her profusely and hang up.

"Yes!" I yell, throwing my arms into the air. I quickly call Liz and am amazed at her generosity. After talking less than five minutes, she agrees to let us stay in her home, sight unseen. I'm touched by how disasters bring people together in unusual ways. Conventional defenses drop and hearts and homes open to strangers.

"If y'all are comin' this far to take care of animals, y'all must be good people." Liz laughs. I promise to call her as soon as we get to Louisiana. Apparently my synapses aren't firing properly. In my desperation and excitement at having found somewhere to stay, the fact that the house is over an hour's drive from the animal shelter in Gonzales doesn't faze me.

My friend and fellow animal advocate, Bland Nesbit, calls. I give her the good news and we chat excitedly. We're eager to set off on the adventure and begin rattling off details and making a list of things we need to take and to do before we leave. We plan everything possible to the most minor detail.

"Jeez . . ." Bland says, flustered. "I forgot to tell you, Jan wants to come along, too."

"Excellent!"

I'm happy that she'll be joining us. Although Jan Panico is petite in stature, she can definitely carry a load. She's also a phenomenal artist with a unique talent for painting cats and dogs. In keeping with the artist stereotype, Jan has been known at times to be somewhat absent-minded. She has a tendency to mix-up words, like the time she applied for a Colorado driver's license. She had every intention of asking the safety officer if he wanted to see her Virginia license . . . but she asked him if he wanted to see her *vagina* license.

Everything is in place. The only unknown: what we'll encounter when we get to Louisiana.

I don't sleep well that night and the next day dawns early. The sun is just rising when I get out of bed, make a cup of tea and sit in my nightgown making another list. It will be a day full of errands and a flurry of activities. People think I'm kidding when I tell them I have "chemo brain" if I've forgotten something. I'm not. It is a fact that people who have had chemotherapy sometimes experience episodes of short-term memory loss. I have stood in front of a co-worker and been at a loss for their name. So lately, lists rule my life. I have a long one for today.

We have each been limited to twenty pounds of luggage by Katheryn's pilot, Steve. I'm uncomfortable flying on large commercial jets, and I can't begin to describe my fear of having to fly in a small Cessna. I take a deep breath to try to alleviate my rising apprehension. I cannot and will not let fear get in my way. *Carpe diem.* I remind myself and let out the breath.

I call both my oncologist and regular doctor and receive their initially hesitant approvals to visit the disaster area. Neither is overjoyed that I'm traveling to a potentially disease-laden area so soon after my chemotherapy. They both remind me of my weakened immune system. My body still bears damage, internally, from the months of poison coursing through it. Sensing my determination, they relent and encourage me to make the best of the journey. I squeeze my eyes shut as I'm given the recommended tetanus and hepatitis shots, and then ask for a few valium to help me overcome my fear of flying—and anything else that might rattle me as I head into the unknown.

Evening falls. As I pack, I meticulously measure and weigh everything I'm taking with me. I continue to pare things down until I only have eighteen pounds of luggage. Heaven forbid that we're two pounds overweight and the plane goes down. Bland and I talk and she assures me that she has done the same. She isn't motivated by a fear of flying, but by following the pilot's orders to a T. Bland is both organized and obedient.

It is later than I want but still fairly early when I finally make my way to bed. My mind races. I never sleep well the night before I have to fly, but this night, I'm particularly restless. I toss and turn and cannot find a comfortable position. I hear every noise, both inside and outside, and every breath that my dogs take next to me on the bed. I move closer to Hannah and put my head on her chest. I feel her body rise and fall with each breath. I pick up her paw, as I always do, and smell it. Puppy breath and dog paws are two of my favorite smells. I stroke Hannah's head, thinking about the dogs I will see over the course of the next ten days. I hope it won't be traumatic. I try to envision what the shelter will look like but can't. I have no clue. I finally fall asleep to images of injured and frightened dogs staring at me out of wire kennels. I wake up every couple of hours, anxious and frustrated that I can't sleep.

I try not to fight it. That only makes it worse.

The next morning arrives and I'm up an hour earlier than I need to be. The sun is just beginning to rise. My three dogs raise their heads in unison, look at me curiously and lay their heads back down. It's too early for them to be bothered with anything. I gaze at them as they sleep peacefully. It tugs on my heart. I will miss them. I rarely leave them and so have become accustomed to them traveling with me. There is something very calming and right with the world when we travel together. I am complete. But not this time. I have enlisted my brother, Michael, to come and stay with them for the ten days I'll be gone. They love Michael— he was their official sitter during my hospitalizations over the past year. This will be a longer absence, and I have to repeatedly remind myself that I am the one who will take it the hardest. Dogs live so completely in the moment. They don't feel the increasing, heart-tugging apprehension as I get closer to leaving them. They will barely take notice of my absence until the door opens and I return to them. That's when the happiness is permeable as they bound to greet me, barking, bucking and bouncing off me with glee. I feel a need to explain to them why I must go and leave them for so long. It's really for me. So I can remind myself why I have to leave them.

I walk over and put my face next to Hannah's nose so I can feel and smell her breath. I kiss her gently as I do my other two dogs, Hanuman, a large male Rottweiler, and Bella, a black Border Collie-Lab mix. They aren't at all interested in me at this early hour and only want to sleep. I move back over to Hannah and lay on the bed next to her. She opens a sleepy eye, sees it is me, and closes her eye again. In a whisper, I explain that I have to leave them and go help the poor dogs and cats caught in the terrible flooding in New Orleans. I tell her that she and Hanuman and Bella are so lucky to be in a home where they are loved so much, have big, dry, comfy beds to sleep on, go on hikes in the mountains and get lots of treats. As I tell her about the poor starving and abandoned dogs, I imagine a scene. What if it were she? Wouldn't she be so happy to have someone there to help her? I cannot bare the images my words conjure up as I visualize the three of them tied on a porch and abandoned in the floodwaters, hungry and frightened. The thought brings tears to my eyes. Instead of motivating me to get up and go, it makes me want to lay there for a few minutes more. I listen to Hannah's deep breathing, which is now bordering on snoring, until I finally have to tear myself away from this warm, safe and peaceful place. With them.

Dressed and ready to go, I sip the last of my tea and stare at the mountains. I haven't yet left and I already miss being home. I pick up my bag and head out the door feeling melancholy.

My friend and our fourth adventurer, Melinda Goldrich, and I meet Bland at her car. As we get in, I immediately eye Melinda's luggage.

"We're only supposed to have twenty pounds each. It looks like you packed for a long vacation," I chide Melinda, only half-joking. I hope a little humor will mask my distress. She isn't amused and ignores me. I pout, wondering how she could be so careless as to disobey the pilot's order.

Finally, she responds. "I weighed it. Chill out. It might be over twenty pounds but not by much."

"Then you'll have to get rid of some stuff." I'm adamant, my concern no longer veiled. "Steve said no more than twenty pounds each."

She looks at me as if I have lost my mind. Maybe I have, at least temporarily. Fear of flying does that to me. Clearly perturbed, Melinda takes bags of trail mix, snacks and a couple bottles of water out of her bag and tosses them onto the floor of the car. Bland gives me a sideways glance and purses her lips to stifle a giggle. We head to the awaiting plane, picking up Jan on the way.

Arriving at Rifle Airport, we walk through the small terminal, chatting nervously about the latest Katrina news, our flight ahead and our mutual apprehensions. We walk onto the tarmac and I stop cold in my tracks. In front of me is not the sleek Gulfstream I envisioned, but an older twin-engine Cessna. My disappointment isn't elitist, only a warped sense that jets are safer than twin engines. Maybe it's because they get you to your destination faster. Not wanting to seem unappreciative, I put on my best game face.

I look at Bland and smile. "Carpe diem?"

It is a question, not a statement. She laughs and watches me dig in my bag for a valium. An hour into my adventure, I've already used up one of only two valiums I brought with me.

Steve loads our bags onto the plane, we pose for a group picture, board the Cessna and take off for Louisiana, via Santa Fe . . . and Baytown . . . and Beaumont.

The flight to Santa Fe is calm and somewhat uneventful, given that none of us, except Steve, are overly excited about flying in the small plane. It is a beautiful, cloudless day, and as we soar over the foothills and mesas of southern Colorado, my valium kicks in and I actually begin to relax and enjoy the stunning views. The red rock cliffs and outcroppings are amazingly picturesque from where I sit. Far below me, a river winds along its lonely course, pine trees hugging the banks. The red cliffs and mesas disappear, replaced with tree-covered foothills. The foothills quickly transition into flat farmland and ranches as we cross the border into New Mexico. We begin our descent and fly over the familiar red rock hills just north of Santa Fe. We're about to meet Katheryn, the kind benefactor of the plane.

Chapter 4

WE DECIDE TO GET OFF the plane to wait for Katheryn's arrival. After waiting patiently for almost a half hour, I finally see an older sedan drive across the tarmac. As the car stops in front of us, I'm taken aback when a tall, blond woman with large breasts and a very low cut dress emerges. I divert my eyes and silently chastise myself for zeroing in on her breasts. I seem to focus on breasts these days. I long for mine, since they were taken from me so abruptly. I am conscious of the two round implants stitched neatly into my chest, still strangers, and have to stop the tears welling in my eyes.

Katheryn is dressed in hot pink from head to toe. Hot pink high heels, dress, and purse. Big hot-pink hoop earrings and pink sunglasses complete her outfit. If this doesn't give pause for concern, she adds to it a bright, white neck brace.

The four of us stand staring, our mouths slightly agape. Bland is the first to get her wits about her. She nudges me and walks over to the car to greet Katheryn. Still somewhat bewildered, Melinda, Jan and I quickly fall in behind, thanking Katheryn for flying us to Louisiana. She barely acknowledges us or the conversation and starts to unpack the car. The first items out, of course, are two large hot pink plastic suitcases, Barbie-doll style. *Way over twenty pounds,* is my first thought. To our further amazement and my horror, Katheryn flings the back doors open and pulls out every type and size of dog crate and pet carrier available, big plastic ones, little metal compact models, and collapsible, tent-like dog carriers made of canvass. She then pulls carry bags and groceries from the trunk. I quickly try to tally the poundage of each item she unloads. Busy calculating, I'm only vaguely aware that Katheryn seems to slur slightly as she issues orders.

I look at Jan standing next to me. "Did she slur or is it her accent?"

Jan shrugs, her eyes still wide and slightly dazed by everything. She smiles and, as ordered, picks up some bags and heads for the plane.

Melinda rolls her eyes and picks up a bag. Looking at me, she nods toward the stack of luggage. "I could have brought my trail mix!" Still clearly perturbed.

Hot flashes ripple through my body as I watch Steve stuff, unstuff, reorganize and restuff bags into the small luggage hold. I can't tell if it's the stifling New Mexico heat, the side-effects of my cancer medication, or sheer nervousness, but I break out in a sweat. I'm on the verge of tears as I watch more and more weight being packed into the small plane. My valium seems to have worn off, and fear has set in. My mind races with nonsensical questions. *What am I doing getting on this plane? Why am I going into a disaster area? I have no knowledge of or experience in working disaster areas. Am I strong enough? Physically? Emotionally? Should I just turn around and go home?*

Fear seems to feed on fear; I am now scared out of my wits. I take deep breaths and struggle to replace my heightened anxiety with positive thoughts. *Be brave, live life, carpe diem,* I repeat over and over as I climb the steps of the plane.

It is only as we're boarding the plane that Bland musters up the courage to pose the question we've all been desperate to ask: "Why the neck brace, Katheryn? What happened?"

"I fell off my horse a couple days ago," Katheryn replies. "I really hurt myself . . . I have to take pain pills and I have to . . ."

Her voice trails off. Bland, Melinda, Jan and I stare at her, temporarily suspended in time as we wait for her to finish her sentence. What exactly is it she has to do? But that's it, the end of her story. The four of us exchange bewildered glances.

Concerned, we're helpless to do anything about her unusual behavior. The plane engines whine loudly. We taxi down the runway and are airborne once again.

Our flight is interrupted with a quick stop somewhere in west Texas, so Katheryn "can pee" because the plane's bathroom is stuffed full of luggage. Once we land, we again take the opportunity to stretch our legs and privately discuss how to deal with the mounting concern we have over Katheryn's ability to work, given her physical challenges.

"What are we going to do?" Melinda asks. "How can she work if she's in a neck brace?"

"Do you think she brought other shoes?" I ignore Melinda's question and stare ahead at the *clack clack clack* of Katheryn's stilettos crossing the tarmac.

We re-board. As I'm buckling up, Bland motions to me from her copilot seat and mouths, "What are we going to do?" I just shrug and shake my head as we taxi and takeoff for the third time.

Suddenly, I feel drained and anxious to take a nap and regain some energy. It's been an eventful, tiring day, and it still isn't anywhere near over. I know I'll desperately need my strength as the day drags on. Within a half hour, the constant drone of the plane engines lulls us all into a sleepy relaxation. A couple hours later, I am awakened by Steve telling us to prepare for landing in Baytown. I'm filled with anticipation, knowing we're one step closer to finally beginning our adventure.

Chapter 5

THE HOT, HUMID AIR HITS me like a furnace blast. Bland and I walk over to meet the rental car representative and hear Katheryn's high, shrill voice behind us.

"I need to go to a pharmacy!"

Bland looks at me. "What are we going to do?"

"I don't know, but there's no way she can go with us." I'm firm in my decision, but unsure of how to handle the situation.

Katheryn's voice grows louder. From where Bland and I stand, we can tell she's upset, her voice reaching a fevered pitch. We rejoin the group, only to discover that Katheryn is upset because she left her wallet at home in Santa Fe. She has no driver's license, money, credit cards or identification. It's been a long day, and the four of us just want to get on the road from Baytown to New Orleans with as little drama as possible.

"I'll talk to Steve. He'll know how to best handle this." Bland heads over to where Steve stands and pulls him aside. Her demeanor is very diplomatic as she appears to be explaining the predicament. I can't hear the conversation, but from the look on his face, it's obvious that Steve knew it was coming but doesn't seem thrilled to have to deal with it.

Katheryn will not be accompanying us. Telling her will be the hard part. Despite everything that has happened, I truly feel sorry for her. We all do. She's a good person with a big heart. She loves animals as much as the rest of us and really wants to help care for them. Given her condition, it doesn't make sense for her to accompany us, but we commend her for trying to help.

It is a most uncomfortable few minutes as Steve takes Katheryn aside and tells her. They argue back and forth, but Steve finally convinces a tearful Katheryn that the four of us must get on the road without her. We thank them both for their generosity, telling them we hope to see them soon. It isn't a comfortable parting of ways.

Melinda and I jump into one SUV and Bland and Jan into the other. I practically peel rubber leaving the parking lot. In the rearview mirror, I see Katheryn looking totally dejected, surrounded by her bright pink luggage. I feel a pang of guilt, but the trip has already taken us twice as long as it should have. We need to get on the road. This might be our last opportunity to get a good night's sleep for the next two weeks. We'll need every ounce of strength to be capable of handling what we are about to endure.

The sun is setting. We start the long drive to Beaumont, on a journey that is beginning to have more legs than an octopus. We've been up since before five o'clock and I'm tired after enduring the long and eventful flight. I think back to my oncologist's words of warning. The damaging affects of the chemotherapy are still prevalent and my body will tire easy. He was right. I'm exhausted. The days ahead will be filled with hard work and emotional turmoil. This day has already overwhelmed my senses and left me frazzled. I eagerly anticipate taking a hot shower, slipping into fresh, crisp sheets, catching up on the latest Katrina news and falling asleep in a comfy bed. Not quite.

The hotel in Beaumont is not the nice hotel we anticipated but an older, economical motel. Disappointed, I'm too tired to be overly concerned. *Okay, minor flaw,* I think to myself. Or did I say it out loud? Doesn't matter. Melinda is distracted as she talks to someone on her cell phone.

I pull into the hotel parking lot. Melinda puts her phone in her lap and looks at me. "This is where we're staying?"

She's obviously disappointed. Feeling responsible for the screw-up, I can't think of a reply, so I stare straight ahead and say nothing. The motel is rundown, the grounds littered. Little patches of parched brown grass peak up out of sand, behind them a dirty, cracked cement sidewalk and then a long line of dingy grey doors. I look up at the second floor. Hanging onto and over the railings are several men and women, sweating in the humid night air. They look haggard. Most are barefoot and dressed in worn shorts and tattered t-shirts. Some of the men are shirtless with big beer bellies drooping over low-hanging pants. Almost all look downtrodden as they stare off into an empty distance with blank, shell-shocked, emotionless faces. Some take long draws on cigarettes.

As we survey the scene, someone spits off the balcony in front of the car, barely missing the hood. Melinda looks at me, her faced crinkled in displeasure. I peer over the steering wheel and look up to see where the spit came from. An old man stares down at us. I stare back with wide eyes, not knowing how to react. I quickly sit as far back in my seat as possible with my head pressed against the headrest so he can't see me.

I pull around to the registration area, get out of the car and am blasted by acrid air that smells of refinery oil. I feel clammy and grimy; whatever is in the air immediately attaches itself to my bare skin. After we check in, I walk back out into the night and am again assaulted by heavy, foul-smelling humidity. I don't understand how people can live in places that are so toxic from pollution. I try to breathe in as little of the putrid air as possible. I fight a desire to run across the littered parking lot. "Evacuees," I say aloud as I reach the car.

The motel reception area had been dreary, worn. The clerk at the counter was tired. Her eyes never left her computer screen as she commented on how lucky we were to get any rooms at all. Every hotel in town is full of refugees from New Orleans. I cringe, feeling guilty for having judged the people hanging around outside. They had fled their homes with nothing and had probably been in the same clothes for days. Despair and apprehension reign. Where the four of us now find ourselves is very far from the comfortable lives we left in Aspen. I think of the thousands of people displaced from their homes and their lives, now living in rundown motels or worse. It is unimaginable. This is something I have never been through, never thought about and even now, while in the midst of it, cannot fathom.

Touched by their plight, we become very quiet. We each grab our small bags and walk silently toward the row of doors. I unlock the door to my room, walk into the darkness and am greeted with a strong, musty odor. I flip on the light and am dismayed to see newspapers scattered on the chair and nightstand. Used towels lie wadded up on the cracked and yellowed linoleum bathroom floor, next to an overflowing trashcan. The toilet tissue holder is empty. The room smells of stale cigarettes and pine cleaner. The bed is rumpled, like someone simply pulled the bedspread up over already slept in sheets. My skin crawls as I realize I am standing in a stranger's leftover mess. I back out of the room and walk next door to Bland's room.

"You won't believe my room." I tilt my head and give her a goofy grin. "It looks like we're bunking together, roomy."

After settling into our rooms, we decide to grab something to eat and pick up provisions for our stay in Gonzales. Melinda is intrigued and happy to find that Wal-Mart is actually open twenty-four hours a day. It's a novelty to her, having grown up in Beverly Hills before she moved to Aspen. It doesn't surprise me that she's excited. There are two absolutes with Melinda: she's almost always talking on her cell phone; and the girl can shop anytime, anywhere.

It's almost nine o'clock, so we decide to eat first and shop afterwards. Finding a restaurant close to the hotel, we eat a quick, unremarkable meal, drink a glass of wine and head to Wal-Mart. We brought dog paraphernalia and our eighteen pounds of luggage each, but little else. Not knowing what we'll be walking into the following day, we decide to prepare for the worst and spend the next hour going up and down the aisles randomly throwing stuff into our carts.

"Wow." Melinda laughs. "I can buy tires, wine and a bathing suit. All at midnight!" She's delighted.

We regroup and make our way through the crowded check-out lanes. In the parking lot, we stand back and admire our swag. Both SUVs are loaded to capacity with dog supplies, gas cans, gallons of water, medical supplies, snacks, paper products, insect repellants and, of course, several bottles of Wal-Mart's finest Pinot Noir.

It is past eleven o'clock when we return to the hotel, exhausted to the point of being zombie-like. Remembering a safety precaution, I carefully back the SUV into the space in front of the hotel room door. I've been told that looting is a very real risk. It isn't that I don't trust; I just don't know. Desperate people sometimes do desperate things in desperate times. I'm not overly concerned, too tired to care and wanting nothing more than to put this crazy, crazy day behind me.

Only after I fall into bed do I finally have time to think about seeing Edward again. Edward is the CEO of a large national animal rights organization. He's also a former flame, one that very briefly burned white hot but didn't have the chance to get past the initial spark. He was the last relationship before my cancer diagnosis, and that diagnosis ended any further intimacy between us. It was my apprehension and his distance. We had known each other less than three months and although I was strongly attracted to him, I wasn't comfortable exposing myself, physically or emotionally. I also didn't think it was fair to drag him through all that a cancer journey entails, especially not knowing what the outcome would be. He might have signed on for a passionate love affair, but definitely would not be there to sit in doctors' offices and hospital rooms with me.

I had called him when I decided I wanted to go to New Orleans. In his DC office, his voice was caring, but frenzied as we spoke. He told me they were desperate for help with the animals. I had assured him I was serious about going, although at that moment it might have been more of a desire than a determination. Still, he encouraged me to get to New Orleans as soon as I could and to try and find others to take with me.

Edward had left a message on my cell saying that he might be in Gonzales sometime in the next few days. I close my eyes so I can better envision his face, trying to remember each detail. His big, brown eyes and perfect smile. It makes me smile to think of him, and I pull the covers up around me and snuggle down into my pillows. In a different place and different time, we might have been so much more. Edward is very much your typical tall, dark and handsome man. He's charming and travels around a lot so I often worried that he might be a bit of a player. He insisted he wasn't. I didn't want to find out. The times we shared together were special, but I always held back, afraid of getting hurt. I wonder what might happen if I see him on this trip. I burrow further into the blankets, basking in warm thoughts. I'm vaguely aware of a queasiness coming over me, but I'm too tired to give it much thought. I write it off as side effects of the grueling and overly-stimulating day. Too much excitement, wine and shrimp, I think as I fall into a deep sleep.

A fierce headache jolts me awake. I feel more nauseated than I ever felt through all my chemotherapy sessions. I lay in the dark, wondering what time it is, unable to see the clock. I'm scared. Once you've been through a major illness, even the slightest ache causes concern. Especially now, less than three months after my treatments, I live with a constant, nagging fear. I'm overcome with anxiety as I wonder if I pushed myself too much. Or might this be what a relapse feels like? I have no idea; I've never been there. I was warned that my system is still weak, but surely that can't be it. I don't understand why I'm feeling this bad.

The nausea gets worse. Trying not to wake Bland, I stagger to the bathroom, feeling my way along the rough walls for direction. I barely make it to the bathroom when I immediately start throwing up. My first wretch awakens Bland. I continue to throw up on and off for the next hour. Bland is desperate to help but knows there is nothing she can do.

She squats on the bathroom floor and comforts me. "Just like old times," she says, smiling. "Your co-patient is right here with you." A cancer survivor herself, Bland had insisted on accompanying me to so many of my doctor appointments, surgeries and chemo and radiation sessions that my doctors called her my co-patient.

My head rests on my arm on the side of the toilet seat, and I turn and try to smile. I know she's anxious, too, and I don't want to add to her stress. Not now, not tonight. It's bad enough that she'll get little to no sleep thanks to nursing me through the night. I stumble back to bed and collapse, pulling my body into the fetal position. I am both freezing and sweating, the once snuggly blankets now searingly hot to my skin.

Within minutes, I throw up again. This time, I'm too weak and dizzy to make it out of the bed.

"Food poisoning," Bland diagnoses, nodding her head.

"Great . . . of course." Tortured by my pounding head, I'm panicked at the thought of not being able to travel in the morning.

I alternately toss and turn and throw up for hours. I finally see daylight breaking through the crack in the dingy curtains. I am sick, exhausted and consumed with guilt at the thought of holding everyone up in this seedy hotel.

The obnoxious buzz of the alarm clock startles me. Bland calls Jan and Melinda to tell them of my illness and the delay in leaving. Minutes later, they join us and take turns bringing me Sprite and cold washcloths. I realize I am too sick to travel, and I'm not getting better. I insist that they leave me with one car and head to Gonzales together in the other. I promise to follow as soon as I'm able.

At first, they will have none of it. I don't have the energy to argue. I can only assure them I will be fine after a few hours of deep sleep. They finally relent. They can do nothing here but sit and stare at me. None of us want that. Their time will be better served at the shelter. Bland helps me sit up and I take half a sleeping pill someone hands me. She puts several cold washcloths and more Sprite on the night table and instructs me to lock all of the locks on the door.

They walk out reluctantly. Within minutes, I melt into the darkness of deep sleep.

I awaken and look at the clock. Just before noon. My white cotton nightgown is soaking wet. I feel weak, numb and dazed but thankfully not nauseous. Anxious to get on the road, I pull myself out of bed, shower and put on a pair of khaki shorts and a black tank top. I throw on a cap, gather my things and head out the door. The sun is bright and blazing. Walking out into the oven-like heat makes me immediately feel drained. I make my way to the car, stop for coffee and Gatorade and head east on Interstate 10. I'm in a bit of a fog, oblivious to almost everything but the white-lined asphalt in front of me, yet I drive with determination. I am on a mission. I'm finally on the verge of experiencing what I could never have imagined.

Chapter 6

I DRIVE THE ENTIRE DISTANCE to Gonzales in total silence, windows up, radio off, completely lost in thought. It is mid-afternoon when I arrive at the Lamar-Dixon Exposition Center. Turning into the facility, I drive past an empty guard station and into a massive concrete parking lot. I feel like I'm driving into Churchill Downs. The building straight ahead is a large brownish equestrian-looking structure with a tall, squared clock tower in the center of two larger wings. Each wing contains three huge, open-air barns. The parking lot seems to go on forever and is eerily calm—all things considered. It is less than half-full. I drive around, trying to shake off the uneasiness that has come over me. I'm not sure where I'm heading, or if I'm even allowed to be here.

I park and stare at the building. When I finally open the car door, the heat and distant sound of hundreds of barking dogs startle me and I stand there, dazed. I don't know why but too often I seem to find myself unwilling to move forward, momentarily frozen in whatever spot I happen to occupy, fearful and apprehensive. I have to make a conscious effort to take my next step, but I'm glued to the spot, not knowing in which direction to head

I have arrived to work at my first-ever disaster area. It's unnerving, not what I expected, to say the least. Then again, I don't know what I expected. It doesn't look like a disaster area, but then it isn't. The actual disaster is in New Orleans, several miles south of here. Still, judging from where I stand, I could just as easily be walking into a dog show or sports event.

I work up the courage to walk closer to the building. I look from one end to the other. It is only then that I notice a long line of cars, pick-up trucks and flatbeds at the far end of the facility. I can't see where the line of vehicles begins or ends, but it is the first sign that something big is happening. Anticipation, excitement and nervousness create an inner force and my adrenalin spikes. My pace quickens. Even in a fairly weak state, I want to run in the direction of the anxious barking. I want to do what I came to do—comfort the obviously distressed dogs.

I reach the building, round the corner and come to a dead stop. I stand, wide-eyed, and try to take it all in. The area is buzzing with activity and I'm intimidated with the largeness of what is in front of me. Vehicles ranging from recreation vehicles and semi-trucks to compact cars cram a small parking area. The entire area is dwarfed by the six massive, covered barns open on the sides and at each end. Within these barns, most of the activity seems to be happening. I glance across the parking lot and am curious to see a field littered with camping tents of various sizes and colors. Lawn chairs and small grills are scattered here and there within the maze of canvas. People mill about with serious faces. Some are in more of a hurry to get to their destination than others.

I'm literally steps away from my adventure, my mission and my desire . . . my confidence sinks. I worry that I have taken on far more than I can handle.

No. I won't let the unknown intimidate me. I can't. I am stronger now. I have faced challenges I never thought I would have to, and here I am. Still here. Alive. Remember, I am brave. Isn't that what I've been told? Am I really? Have I fooled myself and everyone else into thinking that I am stronger and braver than I really am? Determined to overcome my initial trepidation, I begin the search for my friends. I head toward the first barn, walking with confidence as if I know exactly where I'm going.

I reach the entrance and pause briefly. Incessant barking drowns out almost all other ambient sound, echoing off the high, metal ceilings. My eyes dart around the interior of the barn. I quickly calculate that there must be over a hundred ten-by-ten foot stalls. All have shoulder-height metal gates for doors. The air in the barn is warm and musky, an earthy, humid mix of animals and hay.

I walk in a bit further, stand on my tip-toes and peek inquisitively over the door to the first stall. Inside are six large wire dog kennels, pushed up and crammed next to one another, with three smaller cages on top of them. The kennels are different sizes and a bit out of kilter. It isn't a neat row of gleaming, new kennels, but a mismash of old and some rusty kennels crammed into every available inch. Each kennel holds a dog. There's a Black Lab mix, a couple medium-sized brown mixed-breeds, what appears to be a Pit Bull and one little, furry dog in each of the smaller kennels. My first Katrina dogs. I smile, but then quickly see that most of the dogs are sitting in feces and urine. Judging from the bowls in their crates, they haven't had food or water in quite some time. The bowls are bone dry. I glance at the thin layer of wet, muddy straw that covers the dirt floor of the stall. My eyes fill with tears thinking of what these dogs must have endured over the last week. They are brave little survivors. Most of them seem scared and nervous but, all things considered, doing exceptionally well.

I hear whimpering and realize that a couple of the dogs can see me. Their ears perk up, their eyes lock on me, their tails wag and they whine for my attention. Within seconds, all the dogs stare at me, alerted. They begin to whimper, vying for attention. Their tails beat rhythmically against the metal crates. I desperately want to enter the stall and let them out of the dirty crates. I want to comfort them, but can't. I don't know the rules. Instead, I call out to them as cheerily and reassuringly as I can and walk away.

The filth in the crates angers me. Why has no one helped these poor pets? I make a mental note of their location and silently promise myself I will return and take care of them.

I walk the entire length of the barn, passing stall after stall full of dogs of every shape, breed and color. I pass Pit Bulls, Labs, small hound mixes, Golden Retrievers, German Shepherds and a slew of mixed-breeds. The majority of the dogs in this area seem to be larger breeds; almost all sit in their urine . . . or worse. Eight days have passed since Katrina's landfall, and the dogs in this barn have been through hell. They're terribly distressed, understandably so. They have been alone, locked in homes or roaming the streets, scared and hungry for days. Some are injured. Most look thin and scruffy.

I make my way back to the front of the barn and exit into the crowded parking lot. Trailers and RVs from seemingly every animal rescue organization crowd the parking lot. The Humane Society of the United States has a big, air-conditioned RV with a little awning over the door. The window blinds are pulled down tight. The ASPCA and *Animal Planet* have huge semi-trucks and trailers, painted with their logos and draped with banners that flap gently in the ever so occasional breeze. These large organizations are working hand-in-hand with smaller rescue groups, who seem to have little more than the pickup trucks in which they arrived.

I head over to the next barn, passing dozens of people, most flush-faced and soaked in perspiration. Twenty or so volunteers are walking dogs in a large grassy field. They each lead at least two and, in some cases, three dogs. Most are busy trying to keep the leashes from tangling as the dogs flail about exuberantly. I again pass the field of tents and am struck at how the area resembles a refugee camp. I will soon discover it is where most of the volunteers sleep. Unable to find accommodations, they are forced to endure hot, humid, mosquito-filled nights while they selflessly care for these abandoned pets. I pass a temporary shower area fashioned at the end of one of the barns, empty now in the middle of the afternoon. I come to a small, white tent that serves as a makeshift medical clinic. Individuals who are injured, bitten or suffering from any number of medical and heat-related illnesses can get fast, albeit basic care.

In the corner, a woman sits with her face in her hands. She doesn't seem to be hurt or ill and as her head comes up, I see she's crying. Our eyes meet and I smile at her for a second or two and then look away, not wanting to further intrude on her private moment. I wonder if she's ill or simply overcome with emotion.

In the distance, at the far end of the center, I see a gate with a long line of vehicles waiting to gain admittance to the facility. I realize this is the same line I noticed when I first arrived. It seems to stretch the equivalent of a couple blocks. Vehicles are full of animals in various states of health. The check-in process is time-consuming and I feel for both the animals and the people as they sit in the sweltering heat. I watch as a pick-up truck with flashers on quickly moves to the front of the line. Attendants look in the back and immediately direct the driver to an end barn. I'm curious about what is in the back of the truck. Do I really want to know? I decide it's probably better that I don't.

I turn to walk between two of the barns and almost smack into a huge mountain of pet supplies. Every type and brand of pet food, treats, beds, bowls, collars, leashes and toys imaginable sits in this stack, which is more than ten feet high and fifty yards deep. Lined up on both sides of the exterior of the two barns are kennel after kennel of dogs, mostly pure breeds. Some dogs lie in their crates, panting in the heat, but some are up and alert, quietly watching the activity around them. Others stand and bark or whine as their front feet kneed the crates or paw the doors, trying to open them.

The extent of the operation is overwhelming. I could not have imagined being in a situation like this.

Kennels of frightened and confused dogs and cats are lined up everywhere, in various stages of processing into and, it appears, almost immediately out of the center. Pets will be sent in different directions, sometimes depending on their breed. If it's a German Shepherd and there happens to be a German Shepherd rescue group here, then the dog's crate goes to the group's location. If a seemingly healthy looking dog comes in and a generic humane society or rescue group is heading out and has room, the dog's crate might be immediately shipped out. If a dog or cat comes through in undeterminable or questionable health, they are immediately ferried to the veterinarian barn.

I watch as a group of dogs are loaded into the back of a truck and driven out of the facility. Where are they going? I silently pray it is to a no-kill facility. Truckloads of dogs seem to leave out of every available gate and in every direction, as more truckloads of pets arrive. It is madness, a revolving door of pets being shuffled and shuttled out.

Later, I learn that during this first week, no organization could commit to knowing where all the pets ended up. Initially, paperwork was almost non-existent. The first groups of volunteers and animal rescue organizations had their hands full simply saving the lives of the animals. I'm sure they must have tried to keep track, but how could anyone be prepared for a disaster of this magnitude? Then a thought occurs to me. Hadn't hundreds of thousands of dollars been raised by large animal welfare organizations in the name of animal disaster planning? Where is the plan?

I continue searching for Bland, Melinda and Jan. When I can't locate them, I assume they're attending a volunteer orientation. I dread the thought of wasting time sitting through one and hope there's a way out of it. I try to call Bland again but still cannot get through. The phone circuits are either overloaded or out completely. Randomly walking the facility, I can't get my head around why most of the dogs I pass sit in feces and urine. Each pitiful face is more heartbreaking than the last. I can't bear it when my eyes meet the dogs' and I have to walk by, unable to do anything for them. I want to cry for these once beloved pets, now bewildered and homeless. I pick up my pace and determinedly march on in search of a way to help them as fast as I can.

I pass another barn and am relieved to see Bland in the distance hosing off what appears to be a big metal tray from a dog crate. I hurry over and after exchanging hellos and assuring her I'm fine and ready to work, I ask about the orientation.

"Orientation?" she laughs. She looks almost comical, her usually coifed hair in disarray and dripping wet in places. "Ha! What orientation? There is no such thing! Just pick a stall and start cleaning the crap out of the crates."

I'm amused to see Bland like this. She is always neat and pulled together. She is neither right now. I start to ask if she's wet from sweating or soaked from the ricocheting hose spray, but I don't get the chance. She turns and blasts the large tray; the force of water hitting metal drowns out any further conversation.

I cautiously peer in the stall where Bland has directed me. My whole body deflates at a truly heart-wrenching sight. Six large dogs are crammed into crates far too small, and they sit in urine, feces, vomit or what looks like a combination. Too tall for their crate, some must bend their head to stand. They look up at me with sad, scared eyes. I'm annoyed to see that they, too, are without fresh water or food. The few dogs that do have bowls might have been better off if they didn't. Their bowls are horribly dirty, filled with soupy remnants of what, I can't be sure. My angst simmers into anger, so I take a deep breath, close my eyes and breathe. I remind myself of the enormity of the disaster, the shortage of volunteers and the lack of any precedent in handling such a large number of injured and abandoned animals. It is overwhelming, but I realize there is no time for wallowing. I can't waste energy getting upset or angry, as it's better spent on helping these dogs.

I quickly pull open the heavy stall gate, kneel at the front of a kennel and come eye-to-eye with a dog. I'm instantly overcome with emotion, and feel an abundance of sympathy for this little guy. I want to comfort him and take away his fear. He is large with long black and brown hair. He might be an Australian Shepherd or Golden Retriever mix. He is beautiful and I am smitten. He stares up at me with big brown, soulful eyes. I open his kennel door and he quivers with excitement, though timid and fearful. I have to coax him out of the crate; when I do, I speak softly and slowly stroke his head. I let him smell me as much as he needs to, his nose rapidly scanning my body. Sensing it is okay, I pull him into my lap and lay my head on his, hugging him close as I assure him he will be okay. In that moment, I'm sure that I will never forget him, but over time, his face will fade. He licks my cheek and his tongue continues up over my eye. He leans against me and tries to work his way further into my lap.

Dogs have amazing intuition. He seems to know I'm here to help. I hold him and continue to gently stroke his head. His eyes only leave mine when he hears someone pass by outside the stall. He glances nervously at the door and then back to me. I hope he feels safe; he seems to. I hold him and look at the others in their crates, sad that I can't immediately comfort them all. I want to let them all out to roll and play on the straw-covered floor. Instead, all I can do is hold the one I have and again wonder why this is happening to these poor pets. It isn't supposed to be like this. Not in our country. We're supposed to be better than this.

Melinda walks into the stall. As I look up to greet her, she sees the tears in my eyes.

"I know . . ." She shakes her head sadly. "We just have to do whatever we can to help them. Come on, you can work with me."

We very quickly get into a flow, working side by side in teams of two. Jan and Bland work in the stall next to Melinda and me. Melinda takes the dog I've been holding for a walk while I clean his filthy crate. I pull the large metal tray out of the bottom. Holding it precariously so the urine doesn't spill over the side and onto me,

I walk the twenty yards to the wash area at the front of the barn. I turn the tray, dumping the urine and feces into a drain and grabbing a water hose that lies on the puddle-riddled concrete in front of me. I push the handle of the nozzle in. Spray from the force of the water ricochets off the tray and goes everywhere.

I look down. My tank top, shorts, legs, socks and shoes are wet, splattered with a mixture of urine, feces and who knows what else. I've been working less than fifteen minutes and I'm already soaked to the core. All I can do is shake my head and silently pray there is antibiotic soap somewhere close by.

Bland walks up with a soiled tray and turns on a hose. Water ricochets off her tray and sprays her from head to toe. We look at each other, dripping wet, covered with feces-laced water, and burst into a fit of laughter. We both know that even given the trying circumstances, there is nowhere else we would rather be. Being here to give hands-on care and comfort to these animals feeds our souls. We come up with an acronym we will use repeatedly: FBS—fecal back splash. We will continue to experience the FBS phenomenon countless times over the next week.

I take the tray back to the stall and only then realize that I have forgotten dog bowls. Walking back to the front of the barn, I discover the dog bowls are gone. My search for bowls takes me two barns over to the big stack of supplies with which I almost collided earlier. I dig through boxes of toys, treats, leashes and collars before I eventually find two bowls. I hurry back to the stall, fill the bowls with food and water and put the final touches on the crate.

Melinda returns from walking the dog. I take the leash, stroke him gently and start to put him in his crate. He sees the food and lunges for it. He must have been starved. He eats so fast and furiously that the bowl tips over and sends food flying in every direction. He wolfs down the spilled food and sniffs around feverishly to be sure he has eaten every morsel.

I want to stand back and admire my accomplishment—walking a dog, feeding it, returning it to a clean cage. But I can't smile. I don't feel as good as I thought I would. The sad truth is that this sweet pup will most likely spend the entire day alone, only to again end up sitting in his urine waiting for food and fresh water. I've only been here an hour or so but can already tell that's reality. The needs far exceed the capabilities. Resigned, I bend to give him one last pat through the holes in the crate and then offer him a treat from the stash in my fanny pack. I want to know where he's from, where he's going and if he'll be reunited with his owner, but realize I will probably never know and possibly will never see him again. My chest tightens and I feel like I'm going to cry.

Don't get attached! I stifle the swelling emotions and move on to the next crate.

The four of us continue to follow this routine for several hours, unaware of time or hunger. It's disheartening to work so hard for so many hours and not come close to making a dent in the number of dogs sitting in their soil, waiting for salvation.

The heat, my emotions and the sleepless night catch up with me. I feel dizzy and need water. I cross the parking lot to the refreshment tent and grab a small bottle of cold water. The tent is crowded so I step back outside. It's scorching hot, Louisiana-in-September hot. Ninety-nine degrees with ninety percent humidity. Soaked from head to toe, I'm actually happy to be bald. I pour a trickle of the cold water down the nape of my neck.

Looking up, my eyes focus in on a large RV in the distance with a familiar logo on it. Edward's organization. My heart jumps. I've been so busy I'd actually forgotten about him. I remember his phone message saying he might be here in a few days, but never checked to see when he had left it. I stand there and self-con-sciously roll a pebble around with the toe of my tennis shoe, lost in thought. Edward probably hasn't arrived, if he's coming at all. I make mental excuses to fool myself into not getting my hopes up.

It doesn't work. I've never been able to fool myself with that whole "mind over matter" thing. I sense he is close and look up from the pebble to scan the parking area.

Standing in the stifling heat, drenched and dirty, I turn and glance toward the other end of the parking lot. For the first time, I notice veterinarian personnel scurrying about in the barn at the far end of the row. People dressed in scrubs rush pets on stretchers with IV bottles attached to their little legs from one area of the medical barn to another. A vet yells for assistance in getting what looks like a barely-alive Golden Retriever out of the back of a truck. My heart sinks. Emotionally unable to watch the sick and injured pets being carried about, I toss the empty water bottle into a recycling container, grab three full bottles and return to the work that awaits me. The sun begins to set, now glaring and hot on the horizon.

I find Bland, Melinda and Jan working together; I hand each a bottle of water. We stop for a brief rest and I tell them about the medical barn. We're happy the facility has vets and techs to care for the animals but sad at the amount of suffering that surrounds us.

Darkness slowly descends and we continue to work under huge fluorescent lights hanging from the tall ceilings. Earlier, I watched as people with whom we'd been working side by side leave and others arrive to help. All of them probably worked day jobs.

Melinda looks at her watch. "It's nine o'clock, maybe we should call it a day," she suggests, reminding us that we still have to find the lake house at which we'll be staying. We have no idea where we're going or how long it will take us. Only that it could take us an hour and a half to get to the house.

Even at this late hour, the evening air is still hot, thick and humid. We walk to the cars, exhausted, arms on each other's shoulders. We have just completed our first day helping the animals. It feels good. Our bodies ache but our hearts are full. The exposition center still buzzes with activity. We walk past the temporary shower area. A long line of dirty, tired men and women lean against a wall. Towel and toiletries in hand, they wait for their turn to cool off and clean up. The grimy faces remind me of the line I used to see at campground showers as a child. I don't know why, but it makes me smile. It has a nostalgic feel.

My smile is short-lived. A truck rumbles past, spraying mosquito repellent vapors into the air. The foggy mist wafts over and I wave my hand in front of my face, wildly trying to shoo it away. Useless. I gag at the smell and again wonder what I'm inhaling. I'm overly sensitive to anything that might contain carcinogens, and I nervously pull my tank top up over my nose and mouth. We look at one another and grimace, alarmed at the chemicals assaulting us. This is not something we ever experience in the mountains.

We reach the cars and lean against them for a moment, spent, looking back at the facility. Even at this hour, the line of vehicles bringing in pets stretches as long as it has all day. I stare, wondering where all these pets could possibly be coming from. It is hard to fathom the large number of an entire city's animals. Even now, standing in the thick of it, I realize this is probably only a small percent. There are a few other shelters and many other animals still roaming the streets or locked in homes, dying or dead.

We peel off wet tennis shoes and socks to find blisters forming on our feet. The sores don't faze me. I'm so tired I can hardly keep my eyes open. My body hurts, but I find comfort in being where I am with my friends. We chat idly about the day and the pets, and what a funny name False River is. It suddenly dawns on us that our total commute will be almost three hours each day!

We quickly gather our things. Melinda and I climb into one car and Jan and Bland in the other. We head to False River.

Chapter 7

AN HOUR PASSES. FOLLOWING DIRECTIONS that Liz, the homeowner, gives to us, we exit I-10 west of Baton Rouge. We immediately find ourselves on a very narrow, dark road in the middle of nowhere. As we drive down the road, I realize the directions are not making sense.

I'm irritated at Melinda. She's been on her cell phone almost nonstop since we left Gonzales, at times leaving me to drive, read directions and navigate the unfamiliar road. Bland and Jan follow close behind. I haven't seen any of the landmarks noted on the directions, but I easily could have passed them. It's difficult to read and drive.

Tired and frustrated, I slam on the brakes. Dust flies as I pull the car onto the shoulder of the dark road. We're lost, its past eleven o'clock and all I want is a shower, something to eat and a bed.

Liz, whom we have yet to meet, is waiting at the house, having driven up from Baton Rouge. I'm not sure if she's waiting because she's opened her home up to four women whom she's never met, or giving us a dose of Southern hospitality at its best. But she left her husband and two daughters to drive up, wait and spend the night with us, as she would every night we spent there. Whatever the reason, somewhere in this dark part of the Louisiana bayou, there is a lake named False River. There's a house where a woman named Liz is waiting late in the night for four strangers from Aspen to arrive. We have to find her. Neither Bland, Jan nor I have cell service.

Melinda saunters over to where the three of us stand, oblivious to what is happening. "Are we lost?" Without taking the time to answer, I grab her cell phone only to find no signal. We decide the best thing to do is to return to the I-10 exit and start again.

We load up, drive fifteen minutes back to where we exited and restart the journey. It is close to midnight when we finally turn onto Liz's street. We drive slowly down the street looking for her house. We're startled when suddenly a girl in white shorts and tennis shoes jumps out of nowhere and into the dark road in front of us. She's waving her arms madly. I slam on the brakes. I hope this is Liz.

Still waving, she directs us into her driveway. We fall out of the vehicles, apologize profusely for our lateness and thank her for letting us stay with her. I can only imagine what the four of us must look like, tired, rumpled, wet, dirty, no makeup, smelling of dog, hay and barns, three of us barefoot. Bland, of course, had the forethought and dignity to put on her shoes for the introduction.

"So nice to meet y'all," Liz says, her words drawling out. "Come on in. Can I help y'all carry anything?"

It's midnight, I'm tired and she's really perky, especially given the late hour.

Despite her petite size, Liz is a force. She's brave enough to not only allow four strangers to stay in her house but to join us there, sight unseen. She isn't bothered at all by our appearance, but she is impressed that we have come from Aspen to help animals in Katrina's aftermath. Without a second thought, she enthusiastically picks up some bags and helps us carry our things into the house. After giving us a quick tour, she retires to the master bedroom on the other side of the house.

Beyond tired and long past loopy, we feel a surge of energy. We're like four teenagers at a slumber party, suddenly excited and giggling. It has to be sleep deprivation. I'm delighted when every-one agrees to let me shower first. I turn on the shower and start to undress while waiting for the cold water to turn hot. Standing naked, I bend to feel the water and I'm surprised to find it still runs cold.

I stand up and catch a glimpse of myself in the mirror. Some-times, it still startles me, like someone else has crept into the room and now stands before me, a bald stranger covered with scars. It is only me. It still hurts when I take the time to acknowledge myself. The reflection often starts to conjure up the painful experiences, but I always look away and stifle whatever emotions are surfacing. I miss everything that I've lost. I always manage to put on a happy face and hide the hurt that cuts to my core. How can this be me?

I'm suddenly aware of the running water. It still runs cold and continues to do so for another couple minutes. Great. I'm stand-ing in a stranger's bathroom, naked, it's after midnight, I'm filthy and there is no hot water. I pull a towel around me, open the door and desperately whisper out, "Bland!"

Nothing. I creep out the door a little more and hiss down the hall, slightly louder, "Bland!"

She finally hears me and walks into the hall to see what's wrong. I motion for her to come into the bathroom and show her the water. A moment later, Jan and Melinda come in to see what's going on. The four of us huddle in the tiny bathroom in various states of undress and discuss the problem. The water continues to run cold. "Maybe it's so hot here they just take really cool showers," Bland finally suggests, still tinkering with the hot and cold knobs. We raise our eyebrows, look at one another and nod our heads in agreement. That must be it.

The girls leave the bathroom and I step in the tub and huddle in the back, not wanting to get under the cold spray. The water hits my legs and I draw one up and back quickly. Balancing on the other foot, I try to soap the raised leg while avoiding the freezing spray. I cringe and tears well up in my eyes as the water stings my bare skin.

I've never been able to handle cold water. It goes back to my childhood in England. I have horrible memories of being forced to take swimming lessons in an outdoor pool in sixty-degree weather and what felt like forty-degree water. There was no getting out of it. The nuns at my Catholic school were strict. Wearing my white swim cap, red and white one-piece, my body skinny as a rail, I would tense up in the freezing water, draw my knees to my chest and cling to the side of the pool for the entire swim lesson. Other students would laugh at me. I wasn't a popular child, but a painfully shy, self-conscious little girl. My father was in the military and my mother was from Liverpool, so my siblings and I were often thrown into private schools where everyone grew up together, as had generations before them.

I was the new girl. The American. The girl usually picked last or next to last for everything.

The swim lessons seemed to last an eternity. It was painful then as it is now, as I cling to the wall at the back of the tub. I have to get through this hell. I will dispel these childhood memories that have been awakened, just as I will get through this freezing shower. I muster up what strength I can, close my eyes, grit my teeth and dart under the cold water. For the second time today, I'm glad I have no hair. The theme from *Rocky* plays in my head as I pull the plastic curtain back. Like a champion, I emerge from the shower, clean and jubilant. I dry off and put on my jammies. Within minutes, I'm in bed.

I can't get the visions of the suffering animals out of my mind. I think of them back at the shelter, alone, kenneled and scared. I hope they can find some semblance of rest in the late-night hours, but remember the glaring fluorescents and constant activity. I wonder how many people are in their beds tonight, distraught at having lost their beloved pets and homes. It would have to be unbearable to not know if your dog or cat had survived or been lost to the storm. I mull over whether I would rather lose a house or my pet and decide I'd rather lose a house. I can't imagine the depth of despair these pet owners must feel. I think of my own dogs, safe and sound at home in Aspen, and remind myself to be grateful, just as I try to remember to be for every day of life.

My thoughts turn to Edward. I'm excited that I might see him, but I'm also torn. I'm not ready for a relationship, not that I expect to rekindle what we had. With everything I have just been through, I can't imagine being intimate with anyone right now. Although I truly am grateful for every day of life, I'm uncomfortable with what I consider my somewhat deformed body. I haven't come close to finishing the reconstructive surgery or really to even reflect on my options. I'm still emotionally numb, not having yet come to terms with the cancer. It has changed my life, but in ways I refuse to sort through. I live a dichotomy. I'm braver, but more fearful. I have faced death, but am afraid to die. I love life, but can't truly feel what I'm living. It's easier to ignore than to accept what my prognosis might be.

I'm still going through what I call my "deer in headlights" phase. From the day I was diagnosed, I began dealing with things I was being told by just nodding my head and smiling. No emotion. With the exception of the day I was told of my breast cancer, I went through all my doctor visits, my bilateral mastectomy, the news that a few of my lymph nodes had tested positive, and my chemotherapy and radiation sessions with very little emotion. When my hair started coming out in clumps a couple weeks after my first chemotherapy session, one of my close friends and fellow animal shelter board member, Adam Goldsmith, came over to shave my head. As I sat in a chair, head bent down, watching my beautiful long hair fall to the floor, tears finally began to roll down my cheeks. There went my identity, my shield, my beauty. My hair meant a lot to me. I had always considered it one of my best assets. It was a soft, shiny brown with natural chestnut highlights that sparkled in the sun. It was happy hair, the kind that was easy and effortless to maintain and almost always looked good. It was one of the few things I could always count on. I used to hide behind it, literally and figuratively.

Now it would be gone, leaving me bare and exposed yet again.

Adam looked at me and I could tell he was a tad uncomfortable, sympathetic and at a loss for words. As it is with Adam, that quickly passed. "You know Anne, it is what it is . . ." he said sincerely, his eyes tender.

He was right. I have no control over anything. None of us do, really. I will make it or I will not. It isn't up to me. It never was.

Chapter 8

I AWAKEN TO THE SOUND of Bland quietly cursing the cold water. I'm in that space between sleep and consciousness, where reality and dreams merge. My thoughts are blurred and it takes me a moment to remember where I am. I slowly open one eye and find myself engulfed in a sea of pink flowers and ruffles. It's early and the colors too bright for my tired eyes.

I pull the covers up over my head. I want to sleep for another three hours. Every muscle in my body aches and I can't bear the thought of the cold water again. I know I have to get up. We have to be on the road early so we can get to the shelter by nine o'clock.

My thoughts drift to the dogs that are waiting for our help and I quickly throw the blankets back and roll out of bed. Rifling through my bag for the coolest clothes I can find, I settle on a camisole top and shorts. My sad-looking tennis shoes sit by the bedroom door, still wet, rumpled and muddy from the day before. Remembering the blisters they caused, I slide into flip-flops and throw on a pink baseball cap. In the kitchen, I'm greeted by Liz, wide-eyed and perky. There is something about her that is, quite simply, adorable.

"Y'all want some coffee?" She asks. I look behind me. I'm the only one in the room with her.

"Love some." I slide into a chair. I'm only slightly bitter. She's probably in such a good mood because she had a hot shower the night before.

"Did Y'all meet Hootie?" she sings out.

"As in 'and the Blowfish'?" I can't resist.

Liz looks at me blankly for a moment then turns and scoops up an orange tabby. She proudly introduces her rescued cat, Hootie. Jan and Bland walk into the kitchen. As Liz pours more coffee we engage in a few minutes of polite conversation, so polite that not one of us mentions the cold water.

Melinda returns from her morning jog. Time to head out. We collect our provisions for the day ahead—water, band-aids, sunscreen, cell phones, pens, snacks, maps, sunglasses, hats and more water. We walk outside and are taken aback by the stunning view we missed in the darkness the night before. In front of us is a beautiful lake shrouded in morning mist. Thick Spanish moss hangs from tall trees, so reminiscent of life in the South. It forms something of an enchanting arch that leads to an inviting dock. Two empty chairs slowly rock in the morning breeze. The tranquil scene seduces me. It beckons me. I'm torn. I envision myself sitting on the dock, sipping tea, mesmerized by the stillness of the morning water. I close my eyes and feel the breeze on my sunburned face. I'm lost in this tempting escape.

"Let's go!" Bland's voice shatters the air and pulls me off the dock and out of my fantasy. We join Melinda and Jan in the idling SUV.

The early morning sun creeps gently up the horizon as we begin our drive. We're quiet, taking in the charming scenery. We drive down a narrow lane, winding our way through the Louisiana countryside. There are small, quaint, white clapboard churches every mile or so, interrupted only by huge fields of what appears to be cotton. I'm captivated by the calmness of it all. Crops sway seductively in fields that seem to go on forever. I never thought of Louisiana as having countryside. Bayous and Bourbon Street, but not the scenic area we're driving through. It isn't a stunning beauty like the mountains back home, but a peaceful simplicity, the essence of country life.

We reach the Interstate and almost immediately find ourselves on a long bridge crossing a stretch of bayou, also missed in the darkness of the night before. Dead, black trees rise out of the misty swamp waters, creating a ghostly atmosphere. It is a far cry from the crisp mountain mornings to which I've grown accustomed in Colorado. I shudder, remembering fictitious stories of things that happen in the isolated backwaters. We drive for miles and eventually I become intrigued by the beauty of the bayou. I stare out the window, absorbed by all I see.

The soft ringing of my cell phone disrupts the moment. Edward. I pretend to fumble for the phone. I purposely let the call go to voicemail. I'm not ready to speak to him and certainly not in the car where everyone can hear every word.

"Darn, missed it." I feign disappointment and look at the phone display.

Melinda gives me a quizzical look. "Edward," I add.

I turn and continue staring out the window, afraid of what my face might show. Another dichotomy. I definitely want to see Edward, but I'm not ready to face him. At least for the moment, avoidance is the easiest way out. It isn't like it was before . . . at least in my mind. When we first met, I was the picture of health, feeling good and looking much better than I do at the moment.

My mind wanders back to that night. We met at a cocktail party at my good friend Cheryl's home in Aspen. Edward had just been promoted to CEO of the organization for which he worked. The party was held in his honor, to introduce him to our community. I spent most of the day hiking in the mountains, was tired and didn't really feel like socializing. I motivated myself into going by telling myself I'd stay an hour, tops. It was a rare warm summer evening so I slipped into a sundress and heels, grabbed a pashmina and headed to the party.

When I arrived, the crowd was thin. I was immediately taken with this tall, dark-eyed and strikingly handsome guy. Instant chemistry formed between us. As the evening wore on, we flirted with each other. When it was time to leave, Edward and one of my best friends from the animal shelter, Seth, both offered to walk me to my car. Edward and I walked while Seth rode his pink bike in slow circles around us, Pee-Wee Herman style. The three of us were deep in discussion about the bears that frequent the streets of Aspen. Edward couldn't fathom bears roaming the streets. He was excited at the prospect of seeing one, so we all hoped we'd run into one for him.

Out of nowhere, Seth took it upon himself to try and hook up Edward and me.

"You two should go to the Nell for drinks," he suggested, a little too obvious.

Edward was still distracted, looking for bears. I shot Seth a harsh, squinty-eyed look that said "shut-up!" "I'm not going to the Nell, Seth, it's late and I'm tired." I truly was. It had been a long day and already a longer night than I planned.

He persisted, despite my threatening looks. "No, really, you both look so nice. You should have a drink at the Nell and then show Edward around town."

I was tired but, truth be told, I wasn't ready to say goodnight to Edward. I guess he wasn't either, so the two of us headed to the Little Nell, a popular but quiet hotel at the base of the mountain, for a drink and some alone time. Within minutes, we were snuggled in a big comfy couch sipping wine, deep in conversation. I was happy and carefree. For the first time in a long time, I was actually enjoying the conversation we shared.

Lately, most dates left me bored, eyes glazed over and desperate for the evening to end. Edward was different. He was handsome, fun to be with and we both loved animals and talked about them non-stop. He was a guy I could fall for, fast and hard. The evening ended with a quick but passionate make-out session in my car. I dropped him off at his hotel. He asked if it would be okay if he changed his flight the next morning and stayed another day with me. Smiling, I assured him it was. We shared a tender kiss and said good night. I continued to smile all the way home.

The next morning, Edward checked out of his hotel and we spent the entire day hanging out. We began with a wonderfully romantic breakfast at a little café on Main Street, surrounded by jagged mountains rising up against a crystal clear, deep blue sky. We walked around town, stopping to steal a quick kiss or two on the sidewalk, neither one of us caring who might be watching. We both smiled all day, goofy smiles of fools not in love but definitely in really deep-like.

At the time, I lived in a little wood-frame house on ten acres just outside of town. The house was surrounded by magnificent gardens with blossoms of every color, all in full bloom. When you looked in one direction, you were left breathless by stunning, wide-open views of Mount Sopris, one of the taller peaks in Colorado. Six horses lazily grazed in a meadow in the opposite direction, their solid white, chestnut and deep black coats vivid against the bright green grass. Hidden behind the house, in the distance, a lonely, one-lane road meandered through rolling, pine tree-covered hills.

After spending most of the morning in town, we returned to my house and sat on the deck, closing our eyes and enjoying the afternoon sun on our faces.

Edward opened one eye and looked at me. "You know, you live in a little piece of paradise here."

I smiled. He was right. It was idyllic.

Dinner that night was as romantic as the day. Returning home, we walked across the sprawling lawn to the neighboring meadow, stood in the wet grass and looked up at the stars. They were more beautiful than I ever remember them to be. It's funny how everything good seems amplified when you're in a content, happy place. The evening air was cold and crisp against my skin. It smelled of trees and the pasture next door, an earthy, woodsy mix of pine and hay with a lingering sweetness from the gardens nearby. We stood in the dark of night under the expansive sky blanketed with stars and held each other. His heartbeat against my cheek was comforting and I smiled. I felt warm and safe.

The next morning came far too early. Edward had a seven o'clock flight. Throughout the drive to the airport, he kept asking me to come with him. He was flying to a business associate's ranch in Montana for the weekend. I desperately wanted to go with him—but didn't. I had company arriving that afternoon. Suddenly, all my wonderfully romantic feelings gave way to doubts and questions and confusion. Life got in the way. I made the excuse to myself that things were moving too fast and I wasn't sure if I wanted a long-distance romance. I had to decide, so I told him I couldn't go.

Within minutes of him boarding the flight, I wished I had been more reckless. I wished I had agreed to go with him.

In the months that followed, we continued to talk and email and tried to see each other when we could. That was not frequently, but often enough to keep the interest stoked. When I received my cancer diagnosis, things changed. Too distressed and focused on my health, I shut him out.

Now, we might finally meet again in the aftermath of two disasters, one national, the other very personal. With a bald head, scarred body and hard, oddly-shaped implants for breasts, I don't feel very attractive. I certainly don't feel as appealing as I did during our days together. So, given the chance, do I see him or run as far away, emotionally and maybe literally, as I can without being too obvious about it?

As we enter Baton Rouge, I finally listen to his message. It's a sweet one, apologizing for not calling more often and saying he's sure I understand why. He's checking in to make sure I made it okay and see how things are going. He's been in his DC office, working non-stop and getting very little sleep. He wanted to let me know . . . the call faded out. It sounded like he had said "be" and "Gonzales" but the call faded into garble and static.

We exit I-10 in Gonzales, and Bland and I scream out "Starbucks!" In our distraction the previous day we failed to notice it. Bland slams on the brakes and pulls in. Seeing the familiar and popular coffee shop instantly lightens my mood. Everyone who knows me knows that I'm a Starbucks addict. It is my comfort food. Today it brings a sense of normalcy, a contrast to the chaos and despair just blocks away. If Starbucks is open and operating, then life goes on and everything will eventually be okay. With little conversation, the four of us bask in the delight of our steaming coffees. It will probably be evening before we get to sit quietly together again.

The coffee shop is crowded. We notice a few familiar faces, some first responders and other volunteers from the previous day. We're all indulging in a guilty pleasure and, when our eyes meet, simply smile and nod to one another. There are no words shared, but an understanding exists. Far too soon, we finish our coffees and it is time to once again head to the center.

We reach the entry kiosk and are surprised to see it manned. The gentleman stops us, motions for us to roll down our window and proceeds to ask a couple questions, basically our names, where we're from and why we're here. He then waves us through the gate without so much as a second glance. The lax security is disconcerting. We had hoped yesterday was a fluke and today would be better organized and more productive. It doesn't appear as if much has changed.

Walking toward the enormous facility, we decide to work in the same barn as the previous day. Once inside, figuring out where to start, which stall, proves to be more of a challenge. Some stalls contain crates that obviously have been cleaned, while other dogs in the same stall sit in filth. No one can tell which pets have already been cared for and which have just arrived and need attention. The dogs look stressed. They pant and whine for attention. I wish there was a way to let them know they're safe. There isn't and, besides, they might not be. Who knows which of these dogs will live and which might not? I certainly don't. I can only silently hope that they will all live. In the meantime, I will give them as much love as I can.

Again today, no one really knows what's going on and still no sign of any paperwork. It would be helpful to know when each pet had last been fed and walked. Everyone we ask about specific pets just shrugs and goes on about their business. Bland is pissed. She and I could have whipped up simple but critical forms in minutes, if given the chance. It isn't that there's not plenty to do. It's just that we prefer to help pets that haven't been attended to instead of pets that may have just been walked or fed. We understand the bigger picture, but at the animal care level, the gross lack of organization continues and it is beyond frustrating. All we can do is pick a stall and dig in.

Thirty minutes into our cleaning, a red-faced, bespectacled young man in a navy t-shirt bearing the initials of a large animal welfare organization peers over the gate of the stall. Without introducing himself, he asks who I am and what I'm doing. Alone in the stall, I smile and give him my name, where I'm from and that I'm working with our Aspen shelter group. In his most authoritative tone, he asks that I go to the front of the barn for a meeting. I gather Bland and Jan from a nearby stall and catch Melinda as she returns from walking a dog.

"Big meeting at the front of the barn." I nod toward the still unnamed young man, now eyeing his clipboard and trying to look official.

We head to the front of the barn. Over the course of the next ten minutes, several other volunteers join us. We stand, waiting, and our polite chit-chat rapidly digresses into grumblings about the ineptness of management and why we have been left standing here. Finally, the young man in the navy shirt reappears.

"Hello, my name is Brian and I'm the designated barn leader . . ." Brian proceeds to tell us what we already know, that we're at the Lamar Dixon Exposition Center in Gonzales and how to care for the animals. What he cannot tell us is which animals are newly arrived and which have already received care. When Bland politely asks about the lack of paperwork, Brian seems overwhelmed and totally at a loss.

"There aren't any forms." He answers dismissively and tells us to simply follow the orders he's just given us.

Not willing to settle for this weak excuse for management, Bland tells Brian that the current situation is not only confusing but unproductive. Exasperated, Brian's face turns redder as he informs us that our job is to clean dog kennels and not to worry about forms or paperwork. He obviously means well, but is completely clueless and, it appears, in a little over his head.

I look around at the faces of the volunteers gathered with us. It is clear that frustrations are mounting. However, in this moment, concern for the dogs is more pressing than concern about paperwork or our frustration, so we return to cleaning crates.

By early afternoon, Bland, Melinda, Jan and I decide to head to the food tent to reenergize. As we cross the parking area, we see that, overall, the facility is much the same today as it was yesterday, chaotic and stiflingly hot. In the distance, through heat waves bouncing off the concrete, the ever-present long line of vehicles continues to move slowly, bringing pets into the facility. The line doesn't even faze me anymore; I'd be surprised if there wasn't one.

The casualness of my idle thought alarms me and I catch myself. It's far too soon to be insensitive or jaded. The animals need us and we need to be there and mentally present to their plight. This is no time to replace passion with complacency. Each one of these animals was someone's pet. They deserve loving, personal care and attention. It isn't fair for them to be herded together and shipped out like livestock going to slaughter.

It's now been over a week since the hurricane hit and the levees broke. Stories abound about what the first-responder volunteers on the streets of New Orleans are encountering—and they are shocking. I can't bear to listen to the stories of dead animals . . . and dead bodies. I try not to be callous, but as I hear story after story, I realize I'm becoming desensitized to the stories of people suffering, injured pets and the disaster as a whole. I'm becoming used to many things that, just a day or two earlier, would have brought me to my knees. I remember the television images I watched from home. Things now can only be worse in the flooded areas where, in some cases, death replaces desperation.

We reach the food tent and mill about grabbing warm yogurt, stale peanut butter crackers and over-ripe fruit from over-flowing piles. I stand in line for a drink and overhear several people vehemently expressing frustration and displeasure at how disorganized things are. Bland, Melinda and I walk over and unabashedly join in the conversation. Bland asks the volunteers how long they've been here. Most are more than willing to share their experience with us. One young couple recounts how they spent days driving from Oregon, wanting only to help the animals in need. They're clearly annoyed and openly vent their frustration. They reiterate what we already know. Nobody seems to know what's going on, everybody claims to be in charge, and nobody wants to listen to anyone's ideas. They're both extremely upset and tell us how they've seen some of the animals being mistreated. I don't know what to say to them. In this place, mistreatment is a colossal gray area, and I don't get a chance to ask them what they mean. Everyone, I truly believe, is doing what they can and feel is in the best interest of the animals. However, without clear direction, it's hard to see the light. Nonetheless, it's wrong that these two young people have put their lives on hold to come here and help, sleeping in a mosquito-infested field every night and showering in a barn, only to be treated so insignificantly.

Walking from small group to group, we continue to hear the same stories. Frustrations and tempers rise and percolate throughout the facility. We don't know it, but the grumblings are a portent of things to come. Trouble is brewing.

We walk to a nearby tent, empty except for an older gentleman sitting and chatting with two young African-American men, probably in their late teens. The man wears a shirt emblazoned with the name of a humane society. We introduce ourselves, and he does the same. Charles is the director of a humane society back east. He points to the logo on his shirt.

The two young men politely excuse themselves and head toward the barns. After they leave, Charles explains that they are evacuees from New Orleans who have been hired to do manual labor around the facility. We're surprised to hear that there's an evacuee camp about a half-mile from the shelter, with a hundred or more people desperate for work. In the days following Katrina, Bland and I both raised and donated a fair amount of money, as did Jan and Melinda. The money was sent to a humane society's Hurricane Katrina emergency fund to help care for the very animals for which we're now caring.

What Charles tells us leaves us seething. It is plain to see there is nowhere near enough manpower to care for the thousands of animals coming through this facility alone. Hundreds of dogs and cats continue to sit in urine and feces, waiting for someone to help them. We're all working as fast as we can and making very little progress.

All the while, at the nearby evacuee camp, scores of people now displaced and without money or personal belongings are desperate for work. Any number of them would jump at an opportunity to earn a few dollars to provide for their families. Charles approached some of the facility officials with the idea of hiring as many evacuees as possible to assist with cleaning kennels and walking dogs. The plan would free up some of the more skilled volunteers to help organize the chaos. It isn't a secret that dozens more people are needed to help around the facility. Processes and procedures need to be organized and implemented.

PetFinders has arrived and is in the process of compiling a database to track the animals entering and leaving the facility. They need as many trained volunteers as possible to input volumes of information into computers. Time is critical, and they're desperate for help as the information mounts. With each passing hour, hundreds of animals arrive or depart the facility without the good fortune of being added to the database, where they could have been tracked and, just maybe, eventually reunited with their owners.

Vets in the medical barn need people to assist them in their makeshift surgical and recovery areas. Volunteers are needed to provide comfort to sufferings pet and to ferry sick animals or supplies from one location to another. These are all tasks Bland, Melinda, Jan and I could and would do. Instead, we are cleaning kennels. We have to. We won't let these pets sit in their messes for hours on end.

Charles' plan makes complete sense. It would be a win/win situation to hire the evacuees. They would earn much needed cash and the center would have the help it now severely lacks. We're disgusted to learn that the officials shot down the plan, supposedly over concerns about liability issues. One might wonder why it is a liability issue to hire people if it's not a liability issue to have volunteers working in every area of the center. Maybe it has something to do with workers' compensation issues—or maybe it's an excuse. Who knows? But the more Charles tells us, the madder we get. We're incensed.

Bland bounds out of her seat and puts her hand on her hip, looking at Charles. "Hiring those evacuees to help these animals is exactly why we raised money before we left Aspen. We sent it to an organization that is here so they could use it for things like this! What are they doing with the money? This is unbelievable!" she says loudly. Later, we learn that some of the animal welfare organizations initially spent a small percentage of funds raised for immediate care for animals caught in Katrina's wrath.

Charles nods slowly in agreement, equally upset but seemingly resigned. "I know. There's no telling the powers that be here anything, assuming you can figure out who is actually in charge at any particular moment. None of them want to hear it."

He courageously fought the battle, only to begrudgingly accept defeat.

We talk a while longer, and then start back to the barn. There is purpose in our steps. We want answers. At the barn, we have to again shelve our concerns and anger to continue to care for the animals. It's hard to think of anything but their needs when their soulful eyes are piercing us to our core. They need us right now more than we need to involve ourselves in the politics of the place. Disappointments continue to mount and, unknown to us, frustrations are reaching a climax throughout the volunteer base.

Immersed in work, our emotions fluctuate wildly. One moment we weep softly, holding and trying to comfort a dog injured, in poor health or terribly frightened. Minutes later, we're laughing hysterically as we squirt trays and feces-filled water floods over us, or one of us feels something warm and looks down to see a dog is peeing on us. Underneath it all, our emotions remain pent-up. There is no time or place to adequately deal with them. We just keep going. There's little time to complain or even comment on things like the horrendous heat and humidity, lack of good food or our physical exhaustion.

Suddenly, out of nowhere, word spreads like wildfire that we're no longer allowed to take any of the dogs out of their kennels or walk them. We're dumbfounded, certain we must have misunderstood something. Rumor has it that, indeed, orders have come from the top that all dogs are to remain kenneled at all times. It is unfathomable. These pets will now be prisoners, not only jailed in their soiled cages but on lockdown.

Within minutes the dogs, obviously in distress, whine as they want to be let out to relieve themselves. The whines grow from soft whimpering to deep, gurgling sounds that rattle in their throats. They paw at their kennel doors frantically. It's horrible to have to watch them and not be able to help. They look at us, not understanding why we don't let them out. It breaks my heart. All I can do is sit with my head in my hands and try to maintain my composure as we wait for more news. The news always comes in the form of rumor or word of mouth because no one really provides the volunteer groups with facts.

I thought nothing else could surprise me. I was wrong. In disbelief, we discover that the owner of the equestrian center has mandated that no animals are to be walked on his property. His insurance company had sent a representative out to assess the activities and, quite characteristically, the guy flipped at the complete mayhem. For "liability purposes," the insurance agent demanded that all activities immediately cease or be severely curtailed. At least this is what we are told and it seems plausible.

Pissed beyond belief, we're unable to comprehend such callousness. We've had enough. A populated, vibrant city has collapsed around us. Too many people in business suits and air-conditioned offices are using the word "liability" as an excuse for their own poor judgments and selfish behavior in the midst of this disaster.

Unwilling to abide by what we've been told, we decide to let out one dog at a time and keep them in the stall with us. We take turns keeping watch. While one of us entertains the loose dog, the others clean the cage. At first, it's fun to roll around in the hay with the dogs, give them tummy rubs and scratch their ears, but it quickly becomes filthy fun. Almost immediately upon being let out, each dog proceeds to go to the bathroom in the hay. In such close quarters, it curtails our rolling around, but doesn't stop us completely. It's heartwarming to watch the dogs happily wagging their tails and pouncing. These are the lucky ones. We know that most of the others are painfully holding it as long as they can and will eventually go in their kennel. Several already have. Looking sad and dejected, they push themselves up against the back of their kennel and try to get as far away from the mess as they can.

Several hours pass. We finally receive word that the owner has acquiesced and we can once again walk the dogs. Volunteers everywhere scramble and leash up, walking two or three dogs at a time. We rush the dogs to the field, only to discover that now a very small section is cordoned-off, no bigger than the back yard of a house in a subdivision. We're instructed to walk all dogs within this small grassy area. There are usually anywhere from ten to twenty dogs being walked at a time. It is crowded, but at this point, we'll take what we can get.

A short time later, we're told to report to the refreshment tent for a volunteer meeting. Approaching the tent, we hear loud voices coming from within. The tent is overflowing and we find ourselves relegated to the back of the crowd. Initially, we're a bit intimidated at the volunteers' tones. Frustrations spew forth and people yell accusations at one of the honchos from Edward's organization, who is trying to conduct the meeting. I'd seen the woman the day before and chatted with her briefly. In that conversation, I mentioned that I was a good friend of Edward's and offered our help at the administrative level. I innocently shared with her that they seemed to be desperately in need of organizational skills and we could help. She was pompous in her response and seemed to resent the fact that I mentioned Edward's name. She dismissed my offer and told me pointedly that she had everything under control. I walked away from her stunned, shunned, disgusted and almost enraged. What planet was this woman on? Not only was she pompous, but apparently also delusional. There was nothing at this facility that was under control. She projected a terrible image for Edward's organization, and I couldn't wait to tell him how rude she had been.

As it turned out, she was the head of the disaster readiness program. It was her responsibility to make sure there was a solid plan in place for disasters. She had obviously failed miserably. Trying to hide from the chaos she is supposed to be managing, she spends the majority of her time sequestered in the organization's RV. I think back and remember seeing the blinds on the RV pulled down tight. Now I understand why. But she couldn't hide for long.

Now, here she stands, surrounded by angry volunteers yelling questions and accusations at her. I look from one flustered face to another, all dripping in perspiration and seemingly ready to attack. These are no longer volunteers, but warriors who have finally cornered the enemy and are holding her captive.

In a condescending manner, she tells the crowd we have no idea what is going on. Incensed at her arrogance, the volunteers become angrier. Like hungry wolves eyeing prey, they seem ready to devour her. She senses the hostile reactions to her excuses and arrogance and unexpectedly becomes meek and submissive. She is now unable to adequately answer any questions being lobbed at her. She stumbles and stammers while trying to answer a question, and there is an immediate uproar of disapproval. A rumble of loud boos ensues. She has lost their respect. They accuse her of being out of touch with the reality at the center and of covering-up what is happening on her watch. Her face turns red and her fear becomes palpable.

I'm not proud to admit that I take an odd sort of joy in watching her suffer. She is being forced to stand trial for miserably failing the animals she has been entrusted to protect. This once smug, brash woman is now at the mercy of people to whom, an hour ago, she wouldn't give the time of day. Bland and I exchange nervous glances. While satisfying to see inept management finally being skewered, it's a bit unsettling. Like a dictator being overthrown, there is an immediate sense of "what now?"

The crowd's energy grows increasingly hostile. For a moment, I'm worried about what will happen next. It is hot, the air is tense, people are frustrated and fuses are short. Some in the crowd are angry; most are frustrated. We are in the midst of a mini-revolution, albeit a much-needed mutiny. A guy standing next to me is taping the incident, almost gleeful at what is happening.

As things reach a fevered pitch and the woman is on the brink of losing control of the crowd, she dissolves into tears and rushes out of the tent. She scurries over to the RV and finds refuge from the crowd. The volunteers slowly disband, most participants seemingly vindicated. Bland, Melinda, Jan and I sit for a moment and let things sink in. In the heat of the moment, our emotions escalated with the crowd's. Happy that management has finally been confronted, we now need to quietly decompress and regroup.

We're a little shocked at how the volunteers vilified the woman, but feel it is justified. If it was her responsibility to have a plan of action in place for disasters of this magnitude, she deserved everything she had just received. I think of the thousands of dollars this woman was paid to be prepared for a catastrophe such as Katrina. Had she simply provided a false sense of security to those that employed her, trusted her and believed in her? A day later, I learn that she's been ordered to take a couple days off, away from the facility. A couple of weeks later, I was told she was no longer with the organization.

The craziness of the day finally slows into the nightly drone. I'm walking a dog in the small area. In the distance, the barns are illuminated and glow brightly, but with fewer people working in them. The food and medical tents sit empty. Behind them, there is heightened activity in the usually quiet tent city. RV generators hum loudly in a mechanical choir. It's around nine o'clock and, as usual, still hot and humid. I swat at mosquitoes that buzz my ears and gnaw at my legs. They're huge. We have mosquitoes in Colorado, but not the size of wasps, like these are. I hope they're not carrying any contagious diseases or dengue fever from the stagnant waters in New Orleans.

The line of cars bringing pets has slowed a bit but is still active. I walk in circles in the small, enclosed area waiting patiently for the dog to do his business. My exhaustion mounts. I have no idea what day it is. They all run together. I rarely even know the time. In a way, it's very freeing to calculate time by whether it is light or dark or where the sun is in the sky. I have nowhere to be other than where I am, and nothing to do besides what I am doing right now, in this moment. Lately, back home, my life has been ruled by the calendar and the clock, a constant schedule of doctor appointments, chemotherapy or radiation treatments, blood tests and medicines to remember to take. I barely had time to think of anything but the cancer I battled. It was always looming before me in one form or another.

In a way, I love being here free of it all—though I hate why I'm here.

I look around. Everything seems fuzzy and out of focus through my tired eyes. The lights in the parking lot are not lights, but buzzing halos of energy fields. There's less activity tonight, but people still mill about. I glance over to the medical barn. It never sleeps. Vets, vet techs and volunteers provide twenty-four hour care to the injured and sick animals. I watch the activity with a heavy heart.

I notice two men walking up and down one of the aisles. They stop and peer into each stall, suspiciously whispering to one another.

The next morning, we find out that two adult Pit Bulls and several puppies were stolen from the barns. I am heartsick when I remember the men skulking about. I feel certain they stole the dogs. The more we talk to people, the more horrible reality becomes. We discover Louisiana has a large, underground dog-fighting industry and people are probably stealing the dogs to use in dogfights. The puppies will possibly be used as bait, thrown into a ring to incite the large Pit Bulls to fight. When this happens, the Pit Bulls grab at the puppy and viciously tear it apart, and then fight over the carcass until one wins. I have a hard time processing what I'm hearing and want to vomit at the image. We're asked to be extra vigilant at night and immediately notify security of any suspicious activity.

I promise myself I will be diligent in protecting these dogs and will stop anyone who tries to hurt or steal one.

Chapter 9

THE NEXT DAY, WE SLEEP in and take our time getting to the shelter. We've heard there are additional Katrina dogs at Louisiana State University in Baton Rouge, where their auditorium serves as a makeshift animal shelter. Anxious to tour the facility, Bland makes arrangements for us to meet with a woman named Karla. She is eager for us to take some of the dogs and cats back to Aspen, as the staff at LSU has received word that their makeshift shelter must close by the end of September. Homes will have to be found for the hundreds of dog and cats currently housed there.

We arrive at the university, find our way to the auditorium and are stopped just outside the building. We must pass through a thorough security screening and be given badges before we're allowed to enter the areas where the pets are housed. We're impressed with how much better organized their setup is than at Lamar Dixon.

We walk along the perimeter corridor to the main auditorium. The corridor is full of cat cages stacked four high, as is every nook and cranny we pass. Restroom vestibules and janitorial closet doors are open wide, displaying more cages. The majority of the cages are clean and all have food and fresh water. Attached to the cages are plastic sleeves that appear to contain detailed, pertinent information about the pet or pets inside. It is a welcome change from the mayhem we've grown used to.

Meows echo loudly around us as we make our way into the main auditorium. The huge hall is neatly organized and surprisingly quiet given the number of dogs in the room. Wire kennels are organized by size with rows and rows of small to medium dogs, all being watched by alert volunteers.

We walk outside and into a stable area where larger dogs are housed. Three or four dogs hang out loose in each stable. They look a bit confused, but are cleaner, calmer and seemingly less traumatized than the dogs at Lamar Dixon. The difference in stress levels here is palpable. It is quiet and organized. The majority of pets leave this facility only if claimed by their owners. I find that comforting, how it should be.

Karla excuses herself and returns a few minutes later, looking flustered. She explains that a disagreement has developed between the head vet and the director of operations about whether or not to release any animals to us. One would rather wait and continue to look for owners, while the other is concerned about having all pets off the university grounds by the end of the month. We're disappointed, yet impressed by their commitment to find owners. Karla then leads us to a makeshift kitchen and asks that we wait while she meets with the decision-makers.

While we chat, the door suddenly bursts open and a woman walks in. She stops and glares at us. "Why are you just sitting there? Do something! Wipe the floor or straighten these counters!" she snaps. She obviously has mistaken us for employees.

She turns on her heels and leaves the room as quickly as she entered. We sit for a second, shocked, and then burst into laughter. There is no order among the chaos we're living. Nothing is as it should be. Sanity dictates that you just go with the flow, never knowing where it will take you.

Karla returns a short time later to find us sitting in an impeccably clean and neatly organized kitchen. "You've been cleared to take a few dogs and cats. It was tough but they relented. We've got to do something with these animals," she says.

Karla looks beat. She, too, has been working sixteen-hour days since the hurricane hit. She's a short, stocky woman who appears to be in her mid-thirties. She exudes calmness. Unassuming but confident, she's the kind of person you want around you in a crisis. Nothing seems to rattle her. She takes us on another quick tour around the auditorium and stables, and we eventually pick five dogs and four cats. We make arrangements to meet Karla and pick them up a few days later on the morning of our departure.

While heading back to Gonzales, I notice I have a missed call from Edward. I listen to his message and discover he has arrived at Lamar Dixon and is looking forward to seeing me. My heart lodges in my throat as I turn the phone off. I am frightened, self-conscious and insecure. I try to hide my anxiety by turning my face to stare out the car window. I hope no one can see the tears rolling down my cheeks.

"What's wrong? What did he say?" Melinda has seen the tears and her hand is on my knee, concerned.

Her kindness is too much; my stifled tears flow freely. "Edward's at Lamar Dixon and looking forward to seeing me."

My voice is weak, but I try to hold it together. I feel crappy; overly anxious and almost depressed. On any given day, I am over-joyed to be healthy and to finally have at least some sign of hair coming back. But this is the first time I have come face to face with the "old Anne" versus the "new Anne," from a purely physical aspect. I have endured and grown tremendously in some ways, but the journey has taken a toll on my appearance.

At least in my mind. "I don't want him to see me looking like this. I feel sickly and unappealing." Saying it makes it real.

The pain deepens. Tears dissolve the brave face I've been wear-ing since we arrived. I'm slightly panicked. There is no way out of seeing him and I must face what I have avoided. I am gaunt, bald and pale, a far cry from the healthy, tanned woman with long chestnut hair and shining brown eyes he last saw. To add to my distress, I don't even have the most minimal of make-up with me thanks to the weight limitations that Steve, the pilot, maintained for the plane. I'm carrying lip gloss and sunscreen. That's it.

Melinda, Bland and Jan are touched by my sudden tears. They're at a loss for words, unable to understand what brought them on. My emotions pour forth and I try to explain how ugly and insecure I feel. I'm afraid and embarrassed to let Edward see me bald. All I want to do is run and hide and be alone with the animals. For now, that is the place I find my peace, my joy, my comfort zone, with dogs and people that don't judge me on my looks. The dogs greet me with that happy, unconditional love only a dog has mastered. The volunteers don't give me a second look. Even if they did, they couldn't care less what I look like.

My friends don't judge me, either. In this moment, I see how good friends instantly rise to greatness. The three of them, who moments ago couldn't find comforting words, now assure me that I am as beautiful as I ever was. I don't believe them, but am touched when they rally and come up with a solution . . . We'll just have to shop! We've been working hard and need to buy stuff, so we'll make a quick stop. They urge me to buy makeup, new clothes . . . whatever will make me feel better. I love them all the more for understanding; their compassion touches me deeply.

I blow my nose and wipe tears from my chin and cheeks. It's hard to accept being cared for, even by good friends. I'm usually the one taking care of things. This past year has been very different and really hard. I've been forced to let friends care for me, to let them hold my hand in public places and private moments, to bring me food, drive me places and walk my dogs. It left me feeling vulnerable. Once strong and independent, I had to admit I needed people. These three women saw me through tough times. I feel safe with them. Safe enough to expose my deepest fears and insecurities, regardless of whether they're valid or not.

Finding strength in their encouraging words, I decide not to

shop, but instead borrow an extra camisole top Melinda h[...]
her. At least my clothes will match.

I snap the rearview mirror toward me and look at my face. My nose is bright red and snotty, my eyes and lips swollen. Dazed, I focus on my lips. I'm instantly taken back six years to the day my father died, when I sat sobbing to my very best friend in the world, Joyce. She was quite a character. Growing up, we were inseparable; in high school, we were nicknamed "Laverne and Shirley." I was Shirley, the dark, cautious, sweet brunette. Joyce was Laverne, petite, blond, a personality louder than life, bold and, as much as I loved her, at times a bit shallow.

She was driving me somewhere and I was crying for my father, now gone. Stopping at a red light, Joyce turned and looked at me for a moment. Then, as if something had suddenly dawned on her, a big, excited smile lit up her face. Her green eyes danced.

"You look great!" she exclaimed. "Look." She turned the rearview mirror in my direction. "Your lips are all swollen and full and pouty, like you got collagen. They look beautiful!"

I stopped crying and stared at her in disbelief. Then I looked in the mirror. Seconds later, I was slumped over, laughing hysterically, a full belly laugh. The kind of laugh where your body shudders and you forget to breathe.

Now Joyce is dead. She died of an accidental drug overdose in September 2003. We had grown a little apart. I was concentrating on my career and she was concentrating on being a single mother to her son while battling the demons of addiction. When I heard things were getting the better of her, I tried to help her. Of course I would. I loved her. Now I miss her. The pain of her death is stuffed deeply inside me. I don't know if I'll ever understand it. How could she have been so irresponsible and thought so little of life? She couldn't help herself. She had struggled but addiction got the better of her.

I got the telephone call. In the blink of an eye, she was gone.

I was shocked and shattered. Her death made me wake up to life. It propelled me to follow my dreams and move to the mountains.

Dad died. Joyce died, needlessly. Hannah, my dog, was diagnosed with cancer and I was told she was dying. I was diagnosed with breast cancer. So much to deal with in a short period of time . . .

Glazed eyes stare at my full lips in the mirror just as they had that day with Joyce. The pain tucks itself neatly away, replaced with the numbness I find such comfort in lately. All is well.

I'm anxious as we drive into the facility. I know Edward is here, somewhere. Activity is at its usual frenzied pace and cell phone coverage is still rare and sporadic, so it may be a challenge to connect with him. I work for an hour or so but instead of focusing on the dogs, my thoughts wander to Edward. Distracted, I decide to take a walk outside,

As I turn to leave, I bump into Melinda limping towards me. "I have a really bad blister." Taking off her shoe, she exposes a fluid-filled blister the size of a quarter.

"Eeeew. Thanks for sharing that," I tease. I wish blisters were my only concern at the moment.

She gives me a face that makes me laugh. I'm temporarily free of my anxiety as I decide to accompany her to the medical tent. Outside, I zero in on Edward's RV, the organization's banner draped over the side, rippling in the occasional slight breeze. I contemplate walking over, but decide to hang with Melinda instead. We walk along and chat about mundane things like shoes and blisters.

Then I look up and see him. Although still walking, I feel frozen in the moment. My heart starts to pound. The beats are rapid and I have to take a couple gulps of air to try to calm myself. My face is slightly sunburned and flush but suddenly feels much hotter, overheated from the sweltering temperature and accelerating emotions. Melinda continues to chat, unaware that I have zeroed in on Edward. I can't hear a word she says. I finally manage to get a couple words out. "Melinda, here comes Edward."

I watch him walk toward me and feel awkward and self-conscious. I'd forgotten how handsome he was. He towers over everyone as he approaches, walking with a self-assured stride. Our eyes meet and he smiles. He can dazzle even from a short distance. Everything and everyone disappears and there's only the two of us walking toward one another. The closer he gets, the more self-conscious I become. I stop in front of him and give him a deep, slow smile.

Then I walk into his open arms and we hug each other tightly. I close my eyes and bask in how good and safe it feels to be held by him, if only for a moment. I put my ear to his chest and listen to the once-familiar heartbeat. We hold each other. There, in the midst of all the mayhem and suffering, I find comfort. Everything I feared dissipates and I feel better than I have in months. If not for the emotionally charged chaos around us, we could be standing alone on a beach with surf lapping at our feet.

I finally pull back and look up into his big, brown eyes. Just as I'm about to speak, Melinda, who had been awkwardly standing by, lets her feelings be known. "This place is a disaster. What's the problem around here?"

"Your friend needs to chill out," Edward whispers to me through a smile, his eyes never leaving mine.

"Melinda, give us a minute." We both step away from her.

Edward strokes my face. He tells me I look beautiful and that he had been worried about me. He questions my being here, concerned that I'm pushing myself more than I should. He puts his arm around my shoulder and I lean into him as we walk slowly toward the grass. Halfway there, the door of his RV flies open and a guy yells out, "Edward, the governor's office is on the phone."

"Damn. I have to take this call." He looks at me apologetically. "Don't move. Wait here for me?"

"No, go. You're crazy busy. I have to get back to the doggies. Call me later. We'll catch up." The words coming out of my mouth are more casual than I feel. But we're both swamped. I'm sure he has a million things to do. It isn't the best place for a reunion.

He smiles down at me, holding both of my hands. "Dinner later?"

"Yeah, at midnight, maybe!" I laugh. "Go talk to the Gov. Call me later and we'll figure something out. Maybe we can all meet up later."

We share a sweet kiss and he hurries toward the trailer. A flood of emotions wash over me as I watch him walk away. I'm grateful for the excuse to escape and be alone. I still can't come to terms with my conflicting feelings. He's a wonderful guy and I should feel safe with him. I want to be with him, but can't imagine getting close to him again. In my gut, I know what is missing. Trust. My heart wants to embrace him but my head disagrees.

I catch up with Melinda and apologize for walking away from her to talk with Edward. We find Bland and Jan in the refreshment tent and I tell them of running into him. They want details, but I downplay the moment. I promise to update them later. I don't want to talk about or think about him right now.

The dogs' eyes quickly replace the confusion I feel over Edward. Within minutes, I stop thinking about him. My hands are full caring for these little souls who can't understand what's going on and only want to feel safe and secure. I want to give them as much as I can in the short time I'm with them. Chances are, the majority of them will never be reunited with their owners. Despite my promise to not get attached, I find it increasingly difficult not to instantly bond with each and every dog.

Melinda walks in and looks at the dogs in the stall, which include two Pit Bulls. She glances at the Pits and then at me.

"Please?" I beg. "Look at them, they're harmless."

It's true. The two Pits wag their tails happily. Melinda looks from one cage to the other, fiddling nervously with her fanny pack.

She's contemplating something, but I have no idea what. "Okay. Help me leash them both up. I'll take them out together," she says, determined.

"Wow!" I'm impressed with her newfound bravery. "Both of them? Are you sure?"

Melinda has, on more than one occasion, lost her grip on leashes and has a bit of a propensity to lose dogs. I'm concerned about whether she can truly handle these two large dogs. "Yeah, I guess. They seem fine."

She looks at me for reassurance. We leash them and I watch her as she walks away, making sure she has a handle on them. It appears she does.

As I finish up, Bland and Jan stop by to chat. Melinda's head suddenly appears over the top of the stall. She stands outside with the leash of one Pit in each hand and joins in our idle conversation. A moment later, there is a loud noise in the distance, startling the two Pits, who immediately try to run in opposite directions. In the midst of conversation, Melinda's face disappears as she falls backwards, crashing into the crates stacked behind her. Bland, Jan and I rush out to help her and she is intertwined in a mess of wire dog crates, leashes and the two Pit Bulls jumping wildly about. Not sure what to grab first, she motions us to get away and pulls herself up out of the mess.

As she gains her balance, she jumps to her feet in a "ta-da" motion, proudly displaying the leashes she still holds. "I still have them! I didn't let them go!" she exclaims triumphantly, grinning from ear to ear. Her hair is messed-up and a trickle of blood runs down her leg from a scraped knee.

We look at her for a moment, shocked and speechless, and then start laughing hard, bending, holding our stomachs. We can't stop. Tears roll down our cheeks, and I have to cross my legs so I don't wet my pants. The Pits jump up on us happily, not sure what all the fuss is about but picking up on the joyful energy. We laugh until we can't anymore. It's another in a long line of over-the-top emotional outbursts, with this among the most positive we've had since we arrived.

We regain our composure. A few minutes later, Jan quietly excuses herself. She's already bonding with an adorable Pit Bull puppy she found, scared and huddled in the back of its crate. The little female is terrified, so Jan checks on her several times a day. She wants to make sure the puppy isn't pulled and shipped out in the middle of the night. Every morning, as soon as we arrive, the first thing Jan does is check on her, afraid she will be gone. She chooses to work in stalls close to where the puppy is so she can keep an eye on her all day, every day. It's painful for Jan to leave the puppy each night, and I know she'll be devastated when she does have to say goodbye for good.

It doesn't surprise me that Jan has become attached to a Pit Bull. The number of Pits brought into the shelter is staggering, and most bear the distinctive scars of fighting dogs. It seems that at least thirty percent of the dogs here are either Pit or Pit mixes. Most are sweet and submissive, although there are exceptions. Some of them clearly have been trained to be aggressive fighters. Dog fighting is a well-kept, dirty little secret; the Michael Vick debacle is a year from becoming national headlines. A local tells us that in the underbelly of Louisiana, dog fighting is a popular and lucrative business. We're horrified to hear more stories of Pit Bulls trained to viciously tear into one another, fighting to the death. All the while, the dogs are cheered on by uncivilized, greedy lowlifes who place bets on which will be killed. I again hear stories of puppies thrown into the ring to prompt the dogs to fight. It must be true.

I hear too much. Each story makes me sick to my stomach, unable to comprehend what kind of person could take joy in something so barbaric. I'm appalled to discover that many "well-respected" members of the surrounding communities takes part in the activities.

It's so sad that this breed has been brutalized, demoralized and had its reputation ruined by the actions of such idiots. The majority of the Pits I've encountered in my life have been sweet and friendly. I rarely happen upon a vicious one. Here in Louisiana, I also rarely happen upon a neutered one. "I've never seen so many testicles in my life," I joke to Bland.

"I know!" She laughs. "What's the deal?"

It isn't just the Pits. The majority of dogs are not spayed or neutered. Working at the shelter in Aspen and around dog rescue groups, it is a given that all pets are neutered when they become shelter property and definitely before they can be adopted out. Most pet owners I know neuter their pets before they're a year old. To work with so many dogs here that are still intact is unsettling. I make a mental note to ask Edward why these pets aren't neutered and to see if he can arrange some wide-ranging, low- or no-cost spay and neuter programs for the area.

It is late afternoon. Out of nowhere Brian, the barn leader, reappears and pulls Bland and Jan aside. "I need you two to assist me with a project. Walk through this barn and take every empty kennel, regardless of size, and stack them neatly outside along the far side of the barn."

Bland stares at Brian. Her face seems to show little emotion but her eyes could kill. She isn't happy that she's been called on to do such a grueling task. It is late in the day and she's physically spent. She quickly calculates that there has to be almost a hundred empty kennels of varying sizes that need to be moved.

"This is exactly the work that those evacuees should be hired to do," Bland tells Brian. His baffled expression indicates he has no idea what Bland is referring to. No surprise that he's completely out of the loop.

Bland doesn't waste her time with him. She and Jan rise to the occasion and start moving the large, bulky, heavy crates. Together, they maneuver each kennel out of its stall, down the long barn aisle, and out the side opening to the end of the building. There, they stack each crate neatly, according to size. They work together for almost two hours, sweating profusely in the muggy late afternoon heat.

Finally finished, they come in search of Melinda and me. We're unaware of what they have been through. I look up when they walk in and my heart goes out to them. Their faces are bright red from exertion. Beads of sweat drip from their foreheads. They look wiped out, their bodies limp like little rag dolls, their spirits defeated. We stand together and commiserate about how unbelievable it is that they were asked to do such a physically challenging task. Any number of strapping young evacuees could have been hired for the project. Bland is quiet, but inside she seethes.

The sun is setting and "Brian the barn leader" has disappeared. He is replaced by Ashley, a fresh-faced young woman. Clearly out of her element, she, too, seems overwhelmed by the task at hand. Where Brian always seemed flustered, she seems quite spacey. I look at Bland, put my hands to my face and just shake my head.

We introduce ourselves. Our soaked and soiled attire creates a stark contrast to Ashley's clean and neat look. Tired and wondering why we haven't yet left for the night, I'm about to suggest we do so when Ashley pipes up. "Y'all need to take those empty kennels and put them in these stalls."

She points to the crates Bland and Jan have just moved. The four of us stare at her incredulously, mouths agape.

Bland is the first to speak. "You've got to be kidding me."

"Beg your pardon?" Ashley asks.

"I said you've got to be kidding me," Bland repeats, her voice showing signs of tension. "Jan and I just spent the last two hours moving them out there. Now you want us to move them back into the stalls?"

"Look . . ." Ashley starts, completely discounting what Bland has just told her. " . . . I can't help what you were told to do earlier. I only know what I've been told to do now. We're getting ready to receive about two hundred dogs. They'll all need crates. Those crates need to be in these stalls." Her bony finger motions from the kennels outside to the stalls in front of us. "I'm really sorry."

Insincerity rings through her voice as she turns to leave.

This is the last straw. The continuing lack of organization finally gets to us. There is no reason on earth for such blatant incompetence. It's really a shame, because there are so many talented people that have so much to offer. If given even the slightest opportunity, we could all pitch in and make major improvements. The evacuees would be in here, cleaning kennels, moving crates and earning desperately needed money.

"What do we do?" Bland asks. She is incensed. It is the first time I have seen her ready to rebel.

"I guess we start moving crates." I reply, calmly. I know Bland is upset. I want to help diffuse her anger. By now, my defense mechanism has again kicked in, numbing any emotions. I also had not spent the last two hours moving heavy crates, so it's easy for me to be less angry.

My thoughts turn to the two hundred dogs that will soon arrive. Ashley was right: each will need a place. Bland agrees. We have to tolerate the intolerable for the love of the dogs moving through the facility. A short time later, Melinda returns to help and the four of us move the crates until almost ten o'clock.

When we slide the last crate into the last empty spot and all the stalls are full, I turn to the girls. "We're leaving right now!" I jokingly command.

"No arguments here!" Melinda laughs.

I'm filthy, tired and so hungry my blood sugar is spiking. We won't make it to False River until close to midnight. We gather together for the walk to the car. On the way out, Jan ducks into a stall to say goodnight to the Pit Bull puppy she has taken under her wing. We follow her and watch as she lovingly caresses her. We know how hard it is for her to leave the puppy here alone each night. Earlier in the day, Jan had fashioned a large sign and attached it to the puppy's crate, advising that the puppy had been claimed and was not to be moved. This is one of the benefits of the complete lack of organization. You can make your own sign or rule, and people abide by it. Rules are arbitrary and ever changing; the longer we stay, the bolder we become. We will do whatever is necessary to achieve what is best for the dogs in our care.

I walk over to where Jan squats, caressing the puppy, and put my arm around her shoulders. "Don't get attached," I gently remind her.

I know it's too late. Tears roll down her cheeks as she kisses the puppy goodnight and puts her back in her kennel. Jan says nothing for the entire walk to the car. For that matter, none of us say much as we trudge along in the darkness. We're working fourteen-hour days, barely stopping to eat, and our emotions are raw. It is grueling, exhausting and emotionally draining, but there is nowhere we would rather be. Despite my stifled emotions, I feel more fulfilled here than I ever have in my life. I am hands-on with these pets, not watching things unfold from the comfort of my home. I see a lot of the dogs as they come and go. I caress their fur and look into their eyes. I talk to them, hold them and immediately fall in love with each one of them. The connection is that fast. I can only hope that they're eventually either reunited with their owners or placed in a loving home. I cannot bear the thought that some of them may not make it. Many won't.

The drive to False River is uneventful. Not much conversation. We're all too tired or too wrapped up in our own thoughts. I think of Edward and feel bad that I didn't call him before I left the facility. I'm angry at the ineptness and injustices happening there, both to people and to pets. I want to blame those at the executive levels for not stepping up and doing a better job. They're supposed to be prepared for something like this. Supporters have sent money to these organizations so they'd have a plan in place. There's no evidence of anything that remotely resembles a cohesive, master plan. I've been in a number of animal organizations' trailers over the past couple of days and it appears that each organization works in its own bubble.

We're almost home when I remember the cold shower that awaits us. I want to cry and silently ponder going to bed without showering. The thought disgusts me. I will have to persevere, yet again.

Liz is asleep when we arrive, so we quietly go about our evening routines. The shower doesn't faze any of us. Are we hardened to the icy water, or numb to it? Are we too tired to care, or too weighed down in our own personal thoughts? I don't have much time to contemplate. I'm asleep the second my head hits the pillow.

It's getting harder and harder to get out of bed. I finally manage to drag myself up, exhausted before the day begins. It's a body-aching, mind-numbing exhaustion. The work is taking a toll, physically and emotionally. I try so hard to keep up but at times, feel like I can't keep going. This morning is one of those times. I want to hang out, take a morning off, relax by the lake. Instead, I put on my bravest face, force myself to get dressed and join Liz and the girls for coffee. None of us move very fast this morning, except Melinda, who is out jogging.

Liz is wide awake and full of energy. She's been up for a while. Dressed in gym shorts, a tank top and tennis shoes, she's leaving for Jazzercise in an hour. I sip the hot coffee she's poured. What is it about Liz that makes you smile when in her presence? She's a petite woman with a gigantic personality. A typical southern belle, she has dark hair and big brown eyes that dance when she looks at you. She speaks with a deep and endearing Louisiana accent and seems a bit naïve but in a totally charming way. Refreshing, always smiling and happy, there's an innocence about her that makes you immediately love her. She has spent her entire life in Louisiana and finds the four of us fascinating and worldly. I find that funny.

She seems to sense we're worn out this morning, and insists we take our coffee and go sit on the dock. We don't argue. Walking barefoot across the grass, the chilly morning dew is like a calming salve on our tired feet. Reaching the dock, I pull a rocking chair up close to the edge, sit down and put my feet up on the railing. I close my eyes and slowly rock back and forth, enjoying the cool breeze caressing my face. It's calm and quiet, a far cry from our recent activities. I don't want to leave. I open my eyes, sip my coffee and look out at the water. It is still, not a ripple anywhere. It's like glass. The clouds and trees, heavy with Spanish moss, reflect off the water. It is unlike anything I'm used to seeing, since I've rarely spent time on a lake in the South. All three of us sit quietly, lost in our thoughts and the beauty of False River.

Far too soon, we are back on the road. We arrive at Lamar Dixon and get to work. Although each day brings changes to the way things operate at the center, the changes are now expected as we settle into some semblance of routine. As with each day, we partner off and go about the work of cleaning, walking and caring for the dogs.

We gravitate toward our favorite breeds. Melinda and I often work together. Whenever we come to a stopping point, no matter how brief, she frequently disappears and I find myself alone. The first few times she disappeared, I embarked on fruitless searches for her. More often than not, I would find her cuddling a Pomeranian. She has grown attached to one in particular. This time, when I search for her, I head straight to the small dog area. I rarely come into this barn, preferring to spend my time caring for the larger breeds. The smaller dogs are crammed tighter into stalls and some share kennels. They seem more fragile and thus more pitiful. I want to stop and play with them but am pressed for time.

I walk past a stall and backtrack when I realize I have just passed Melinda. "Hey!" I call out to her over the stall door. "What's up?"

"Look at this poor little dog." She holds up a growling ball of matted fur.

"He doesn't sound very happy, Melinda," I laugh. "I'm heading back to the barn. Are you coming?"

She promises to follow. As I walk away, she continues to comfort the growling dog. I realize it might be awhile before she joins me, so I take my time going back to the barn. I take the opportunity to explore the barn at the top of the facility, never having been inside. When I enter, it immediately feels and smells different than the other barns. It is calmer here. I'm pleasantly surprised to see that this barn is full of horses. They aren't crammed together like the dogs are, although some stalls do contain two horses. This barn smells good like a stable and I take in a long sniff of the sweet earthy smell. I like this barn. It is quiet, save for an occasional horse whinny. What a difference it makes when there are no dogs barking! The energy level is lower and the horses seem less stressed.

I spend about thirty minutes walking from stall to stall, admiring the beautiful equines. They are a world away from the traumatized pets in the other barns. If I didn't know better, it would seem I was strolling through the stables at an equestrian event. The visit to the barn calms me.

I walk slowly back to my work with the dogs. I make my way to the stalls in which Melinda and I had been working before she disappeared. She's crouched over something. When I approach her, she turns and thrusts what looks like ET up into my face.

"Melinda. You scared the hell out of me. What is that?" I'm startled by what she has just shoved toward me.

"It's the Pom." She laughs at my reaction.

I laugh with her. "What happened to it?"

"I decided he was too hot, so I thought he'd feel better if I shaved him," she says, innocently.

"Yeah, well, don't get attached to it!" I walk away.

I catch up with Bland, who is talking with a cheery blond woman. She introduces me to Deb, a Gonzales local. Deb works at a bank in southern Louisiana and comes to the shelter every night. As the evening deepens, we work side by side with Deb. A bond forms. We tell her we're staying in False River, and she is stunned.

"Y'all can't be driving there and back every day, are y'all?" Deb asks in disbelief.

"There and back every day!" Bland says.

"Y'all can't do that. Come and stay with me and my husband. I live about five minutes away. You have to stay with us!"

"There's four of us," Bland says. "Are you sure we won't be imposing?"

"Heck no! Come and stay tonight. My husband will fix us a nice meal," she says warmly.

"Well, we can't tonight," Bland explains. "All of our stuff is in False River and Liz is expecting us. Maybe we can stay tomorrow night; would that work?"

With that, it's set. We will stay one more night in False River and spend our two final nights with Deb and her husband, Vic.

As we realize our days at the center are coming to an end, the bonds we have formed with various dogs intensify. Jan continues to bond with the Pit Bull puppy who she has now named "Daisy." Watching her, there's no doubt in my mind that Daisy will be coming back to Aspen with us. Her love for the little black and white puppy touches me.

Bland disappears. Unbeknownst to any of us, she has wandered over to the medical barn, drawn by three Beagle puppies being carried in on a stretcher. The puppies are in dire condition, hooked-up to IVs and surrounded by medical personnel. She is absolutely taken with the dogs and follows the vet and tech into the medical area. One puppy in particular is extremely ill. Bland is a strong woman who, emotionally, can handle more than most. When she returns, she tells us about them and bursts into tears. She tries to describe how really sick they are and that the smallest of the three was writhing in pain. The vets are concerned that the sickest puppy will not make it. Bland is inconsolable and we try to comfort her as best we can.

It is upsetting to see her hurting so much over the puppies and know there is nothing we can do. I understand her anguish. It is deeply painful to see innocent animals in such agony and not be able to help them. It is heartbreaking when a decision is made to put one down. When dealing with the enormity of so many sick animals, those that under normal circumstances might have been given a chance at life, are not. Time and supplies are short and many of the sicker or more severely injured dogs are put down instead of nursed back to health. It is devastating to see it happen. We can't linger with the sorrow, as we're surrounded by so many others. We must quickly move on to the next. It doesn't seem fair. They deserve better, and we deserve the time to mourn them. For now, though, we must lock away emotion and deal with it another day. I wonder if it is akin to what doctors working triage in catastrophic accidents experience. No bonding with the sick and critically injured. In the very best of circumstances, all you can do is fix them as best you can and send them on their way.

I continue to remind everyone not to get attached to the dogs, but find myself bonding with a male Rottweiler. In going from stall to stall, when I see a Rottweiler, there is no stopping me. I'm immediately in the stall petting the dog, despite being warned to stay away "because they're dangerous." Many of the dogs are sweet, loving and friendly, even timid.

I look at the paperwork on the kennel of this Rottie and see that he came in with a collar and tag. His name is "Rocky." He had been found in an area a few miles from the Ninth Ward. Rocky is a gorgeous male, about three years old, strong and healthy. When I enter his stall, he looks at me with an engaging, slightly demanding glare so typical of the breed. I bend and talk to him through his kennel and when I feel sure he is harmless, remove the yellow tape and let him out into the stall. The tattered paperwork on his cage notes that a call had been made to the number on his tag but the line had been disconnected. The majority of the telephone lines in New Orleans are down, which exacerbates the entire rescue effort.

The word "Caution" is written in big letters across Rocky's form, but no caution is needed. He is one big love and all he wants to do is to get as close to me as possible. I look at the tag on his collar, take out my cell phone and call the number myself, just to be sure. I immediately get a loud, shrill tone and a recording stating all circuits are busy.

Rocky's kennel needs attention, but I want to check on Bland, so I promise him I will return to clean his cage. I turn to leave and look back at him once again. There is something about him that won't let me leave. His piercing eyes lock onto mine and I feel an instant, deep connection to him. I have always believed that it isn't how we bond with dogs, but how they bond with us that makes us love them like we do. Rocky is a pro at bonding. He stares at me and I'm hooked.

I'm frustrated to find that so many of the Rottweilers, German Shepherds, Pits and other "aggressive breeds" sit in kennels swathed in yellow "caution" tape. Consequently, their kennels haven't been cleaned and are filthy. The majority of them are harmless and don't deserve to be stereotyped.

The first time Jan and I encounter the caution tape, we're standing together preparing to clean a Rottie's cage.

"Don't open those crates," a passing barn leader snipes over his shoulder. "They're aggressive dogs and only trained personnel are allowed to work with them."

By now, I have little respect for barn leaders. The majority are a lot of talk and little action, scurrying around or staring at clipboards.

I wait until he's out of earshot and look at Jan. "Are you thinking what I'm thinking?" I lean down to open the Rottie's crate. "What are we supposed to do, let them all sit in filth all day?"

"I agree. Screw that." Jan is equally pissed at the lack of compassion. She kneels with me as we coax a very scared, very sweet Rottweiler out of its crate. I rip the warning tape off the crate and walk the precious pup while Jan cleans its soiled crate.

Now that all dog walkers have been exiled to the small roped-off area, it has become quite monotonous. People walk dogs night and day, following the same routine. We enter, grab a poop bag and then fall into line, one behind the other. We walk in a slow circle, careful to keep a safe distance between one another so the dogs cannot fight. At night, the area reminds me of a scene out of the movie *Night of the Living Dead*, as exhausted workers walk the circle in a zombie-like trance. Sometimes volunteers will take the opportunity to smoke a cigarette or make a phone call, if they happen to be lucky enough to get a connection. Cell service continues to be an ever-elusive commodity.

Most of us obediently obey the rules and keep safe distances from one another, with one exception: Melinda, who seems oblivious despite being frequently reminded. Bland, Jan or I will be walking one, two or three dogs, usually lost in thought or attending to the dog, when suddenly they lunge at Melinda, who approaches us with three or four little yappy dogs. She is a sight as she fights to control the dogs, their leashes criss-cross each other, and they trip her. The routine of the walk transforms into out-of-control mayhem with dogs lunging, snapping and barking aggressively as she tries to untangle herself and gain control.

"Melinda!" We shriek, struggling to get our large dogs under control, slightly embarrassed at the commotion we're causing.

Nothing fazes Melinda. "Whatever . . ." She shrugs, a bit fed up with all the rules. Regardless of how snippy I get with her, Melinda usually has the ability to completely blow off any attitude and come back at you with genuine concern. She feels concern for me, especially now. She always makes certain that I'm doing okay, eating, not too tired, drinking enough fluids. In the midst of enduring this hell we're in, it is refreshing to remember the deep friendship that binds us.

Our drive back to Liz's this evening is filled with banter and enthusiasm about not having to make the trip again. We also discuss the best way to tell Liz we will not be staying with her anymore. She's asleep when we get there, so the conversation must wait until morning. My cold shower that evening is bearable, knowing I will not have to endure another one.

We see Liz in the morning and share the news that we will be staying in Gonzales the next two nights. She is disappointed, but gracious and understanding. I hope she's secretly relieved at not having to drive back and forth from Baton Rouge again. She tells us she will miss us terribly and has loved and will miss hearing our stories every morning.

During this conversation, we break it to her that the water is not very hot in her bathrooms.

"Huh?" She says, looking at me, her big brown eyes momentarily clouded with confusion. "What do y'all mean? You haven't had any hot water? Oh, no! My husband must have turned the hot water heater off when he left last weekend. Y'all should have told me! We have two water heaters and my side was on, so I had no idea!"

I stare at her, momentarily dumbfounded, at a loss for words. I turn to Bland, who laughs. "Oh, gawd! Is that all it was? We felt bad and didn't want to say anything. I can't believe it. We should have said something."

We're still laughing about it when Melinda and Jan join us, although Melinda doesn't seem to find it nearly as funny as we do. Something as simple as a turned-off water heater caused us the agonizing and frigid showers that we dreaded but endured every night.

We gather our things and say good-bye to Liz. There is a genuine sadness in leaving, as she has been so kind, warm and loving to us. Days ago, we were complete strangers; now, it is hard to tell her good-bye. Circumstance brought the five of us together and we became close friends, only to part as quickly as we arrived. We promise to stay in touch and make Liz promise that she will bring her family to the mountains during Spring break so we can repay her kindness and hospitality.

Chapter 10

WE'RE STOPPED AT THE ENTRY kiosk. A man in a camouflage uniform checks our badges, questions us and then waves us into the facility. It's nice to finally see some sense of security at the entrance. I'm sure it has to do with the recent dog theft attempts. Walking toward the barns, we realize the increased security isn't just at the entry gate. Two more soldiers talk to a group of representatives of the various animal organizations touring the facility.

I walk into a barn to start work and notice things are a bit more organized than usual. Signs are hung throughout the area, especially at the hosing stations, where it is now mandated that hands are to be washed and gloves and masks worn. Next to every sign sits a box of rubber gloves saturated with the constantly spewing hose sprays. Both the signs and gloves are completely ignored by most volunteers, including me, as we continue with the routines we have established.

I take a quick lap around the two barns, which hold the kennels of the dogs we will be taking. I want to make sure none have been moved or shipped out and find all of them in the same spots we last left them. There is a less frenzied pace in the facility, which makes it easier to keep track of the dogs. PetFinders is finally up and running but faces immense challenges in logging as many of the pets as they can. It is amazing grace that they are able to step up to the task of trying to track the pets. Without them, I think, things would have turned out much differently. They bring the very systems to the area that the large animal welfare agencies should have had in place from day one but were nonexistent.

As I complete the walk, I am happy to see that all kennels remain tagged with our name. All the dogs are in place, waiting to go. I linger at Rocky's kennel a little longer this morning. He is so happy to see me when I arrive, and I am happy to see his kennel is in better shape than it has ever been. Things are definitely coming together. I take him for a longer walk and feel much calmer, knowing he will be leaving with me tomorrow. We take a few extra minutes and sit in the sun together. I close my eyes and enjoy the rays while he sits almost in my lap and takes delight in watching the comings and goings. I'm happy to see he is as well behaved as I had hoped. With all the activity and strangers milling about, he is as friendly and welcoming as can be. When it comes time to put him in his kennel, it is surprisingly less traumatic. In an odd way, it seems we both know that we will be getting out of here soon, together. We both find comfort in that.

We again work late into the night until Deb comes to find us so we can follow her to her house. It is a modest sprawling home that sits off the road, surrounded by huge trees with moss hanging heavy on the branches. Once inside, we're introduced to Deb and Vic's dogs as well as their neighbor's dogs, which seem to visit frequently. Deb gives us a quick tour. By the time we've had a quick bite to eat, all taken showers and taken advantage of having internet access, we excuse ourselves to our rooms and get to bed earlier than we have in days.

I open my eyes and am startled. Peering down at me is a tiger. I jerk my head up and focus my eyes better on a large purple and gold stuffed tiger hanging on the wall directly above the bed. As I look around the room, the sea of purple and gold confuses me momentarily. It is a far cry from the floral and frilly pink room at Liz's house. This room has a much more masculine feel, and the initials LSU are emblazoned in the deep purple and gold colors that swath the room. Memories from the night before slowly start coming back to me. I am sleeping in Deb and Vic's son's room. He attends Louisiana State University and they are huge fans. So are most residents of Baton Rouge. The purple, the gold, the tigers and the LSU emblazoned everywhere bear witness to that fact. I lay there for a moment and enjoy the deep, cool, rich colors, but am a little rattled by the tiger eyes staring at me.

I decide to get up and find Melinda, Bland and Jan. This will be our last day at the Lamar Dixon facility and I find myself feeling melancholy. It will be hard to leave, as I feel we have amounted to just a drop in the sea of need. I meet everyone in the kitchen, where Deb is dressed and heading out to her job at the bank. The four of us leave behind her.

The trip from Deb's to Lamar Dixon is so much faster that I barely have time to think about anything. The nice thing about being at Liz's place is that the drive gave you time to gear up for the facility or decompress after another day. This being our last morning, I feel an overwhelming need for time to reflect. I am overcome with a heavy sadness that I cannot adequately reconcile before we arrive at Lamar Dixon. I really want to savor every moment of this day, but it is already going by too fast.

I look at things differently, taking in every sight and smell, wanting to remember things vividly but knowing I will eventually forget most of the details. I know I will miss everything and everyone terribly. It is hard to get my head around the fact that our time is coming to an end and we must leave when so many animals continue to arrive and need care. I have no choice but to hope and to trust that they will be cared for. To think anything else would be crushing and send me into a tailspin. I want to make sure every last pet is cared for, but I have to accept that it is impossible for me, personally, to do so. The emotions that start to well inside are relegated to the vast black hole, my emotional vault.

Despite the utter chaos we have endured, today I find tremendous comfort in the mayhem. I don't want to leave. But I smile, thinking of Rocky and of the opportunity to save him. I can't wait to see him again. I think of all the people here and at the other animal rescue facilities set up along the Gulf Coast, and know that I am but one of many, many people taking these animals not only into their hearts but also into their homes. Many of us are trying to find what homes we can for these pets and thus saving so many. For whatever reason, Rocky has given me hope and made me smile. He has been a catalyst in helping me see and understand all the things we are doing, and not dwelling on what we cannot do.

I decide to head over to where he is so I can once again assure him he's coming home with me. Before too long, it will be time to start the formal gathering and processing of our group. I won't be able to enjoy any one-on-one time with him.

As I head to his kennel, I run into Bland and one of the facility representatives. It's time to start the out-processing. We must walk to each kennel, check each dog, and submit all paperwork to the representative, who reviews it and signs off on the dog. From there, we move into the outtake area for final processing. One by one, we visit each kennel.

When we arrive at Rocky's, I beam at him. He is overly excited to see me and we all agree he is a gorgeous boy. The representative nods in agreement and starts reviewing Rocky's paperwork. She seems to take longer with it, but I'm sure it is because I am so excited and anxious to have finally arrived at this final step. She steps back and stares at his kennel for a little longer than the others, looks at the paperwork again, and then stoops and looks at his collar and tags.

"This dog isn't going." She stands up and starts writing something on the clipboard she holds. I am stunned and look at Bland; I must have heard her wrong.

"What??" I blurt it out without realizing any words have passed my lips.

"He looks too good. He obviously has an owner and I'm sure he'll be claimed." She still doesn't bother to look up.

I am horrified. In all the time we have been here, an exceptionally low number of pets have been reunited with their owners. Yes, the number of dogs coming into and being shipped out of the facility has slowed a bit, and PetFinders is helping to track owners, but the chances are very, very high that Rocky will be shipped somewhere. Why can't it be with me? So many of these dogs appear to be in good condition but are still leaving for temporary foster homes. What is different about Rocky? I can't believe what I have heard.

"Please . . ." I stammer. "You can't be serious. Please, let me take him. I promise you I will do everything I can to find his owner as quickly as I can and once I do, I promise to immediately arrange for them to be reunited."

I am desperate. I cannot fathom what she is saying: Rocky cannot come with us, but will be left here. I have no idea what will happen to him, or if he will ever be reunited with his pre-Katrina owner. I am desperate to know he will be okay and well cared for.

"Nope. Sorry." She continues writing.

I am shocked. I panic. He will not be allowed to leave with us. I feel like someone's hands wrap around my throat, preventing me from breathing. My mind won't work. I can't think. I have to think. Right now. I have to think of some way to get her to change her mind, even as I watch her rip all of our paperwork off Rocky's kennel and rip it in half. I can't leave him here not knowing, for sure, that he would not be put down. But there is no guarantee. If he is left here, I will never know. That devastates me.

I have to find a way to take him. The thought that he could not join us never even occurred to me. Now it shakes me to my very core.

I look at the representative. "I promise you . . ." I stare at her, my eyes filling with tears. ". . . Please, let us take him. I promise you I will find his owner. He will be well-cared for until then. Please . . ."

She finally looks at me. "I'm sorry. No." She turns and makes her way out of the stall and on to our next dog.

I turn and look at Bland, who is almost crying, too. She is not upset for Rocky but distressed that I am in such pain. Our eyes meet and she seems to be at a loss, although I can tell she is concerned. I stare at her in disbelief. Nothing is registering.

"I'm so sorry . . ."

It's all I hear as I turn and stumble out of the stable. I walk, blindly passing faces that turn and stare at my obvious upset. I don't know where I'm going. I just know I have to go somewhere—fast. I have to get out of there and away from everyone. I choke on the pain, so overcome with emotion that I am unable to handle or process where I am going. I am not even aware of the heavy tears that burn down my cheeks and fall onto my chest as I walk, one foot numbly in front of the other.

I find myself at the edge of the facility and sit on a big rock. Elbows on knees, I bend my head and the sobbing starts. I choke in some air as my body unleashes the pent-up emotions. I don't want to suffer a meltdown here, now, but I can't stop what is happening. I sob for myself and the six months I have just endured, I sob for Rocky and what will become of him, and for all the dogs of every breed that have been lined up and shipped to who knows where. I sob for Bland's sick Beagles. My heart aches for the dogs and cats still starving and dying on the streets of New Orleans. My mind flashes with images of hundreds of pairs of beautiful, innocent yet terrified eyes that silently plead to be held and fed and saved and loved. I can't do anything for most of them. My sorrow and feeling of helplessness rip me to the depths of my soul.

I eventually find the strength to pull myself together and stop.

I'm drained. I look up and take in the entire scene from both an emotional and literal distance. It all seems so incredibly surreal. Through the blur of tearful eyes and the haze of the heat, I suddenly feel like I'm in a war zone or a scene from the television show M*A*S*H*. What has happened here? Things changed so quickly. I guess things grew so disorganized that the military was called in to assist. National Guard soldiers dressed in camouflage with guns at their side now ride around the facility in military jeeps. Two chain link fences are almost finished being erected around the entire perimeter of the property. The ten-foot fences are three feet apart, giving the appearance of a prison yard.

I am spent, confused, frustrated and deflated. Who are these people? I hope they truly care about the animals whose welfare lies in their hands, and that this is not just another mission to them. Bland, Melinda, Jan and I have poured our hearts and souls into caring for these pets, along with hundreds of other volunteers. Now, it seems to me, the objective is simply to get them in and out as fast as possible. They weren't individual, precious little beings. They became cargo. Crates being sent off, somewhere, anywhere, just out of here so more could come in.

My emotions are getting the better of me. I try to talk myself through the reality of the situation. That's what has taken hold of me—reality. It has won the emotional battle. I am broken and I must accept that I cannot fix it all. No one can. No one group or one organization or city can fix it all. Our country has finally responded to this immense catastrophe and still it cannot be fixed quickly and without immeasurable suffering and death. I sit on the rock in an empty daze for a few minutes longer and then force myself to stand up to return to my friends. I had hurriedly abandoned them to be alone in my sorrow and helplessness. I can't bear to walk back through the stable where Rocky still sits, alone in his crate, waiting for me to come for him

I take the long way back to the Outtake area to avoid seeing

Rocky. I'm torn. I can't bear the thought of seeing him . . . but I have to see him and say good-bye. I follow my heart instead of my head, knowing I have to say good-bye to him. I turn around and head in his direction. When I arrive, he is ecstatic. He flails around in his crate, rocking it from side to side. Frenzied, he whimpers and yelps, demanding I let him out. I immediately oblige. I barely have the kennel door open when he bounds out and knocks me over into the dirty, wet straw. As I hit the ground, my baseball cap flies off and Rocky proceeds to cover my face and bald head with sloppy, wet dog kisses. His big, brown eyes shine as we play in the straw. I talk to him lovingly and he tilts his head as if he understands everything I say. He trusts me completely and frolics, carefree. I feel guilty. It breaks my heart to leave him here. It is the ultimate betrayal.

It is time for me to say good-bye. I wrap my arms around his back and shoulders and hold him in a tight hug. I squeeze my eyes closed to try and hold back the swelling torrent of tears. It doesn't work. The love and pain are both too deep. As a river of tears streams down my face, I clutch him tighter and bury my face into his fur. I want to remember everything about him, the way his body feels, the softness of his fur, his musky doggie smell. I relish it all. I could stay there forever, but he wriggles playfully and tries to free himself. He thinks we're playing a wrestling game and he ducks out of my arms, runs to the opposite side of the stall and then bounds back to me. He falls into my lap and licks the tears on my cheeks and perspiration on my brow. I far too quickly became attached to this little guy. Thinking I was taking him home was what kept me going some days.

I seriously consider stealing him. I could just take him to my car and bluff my way out of the facility with him. As the plan unfolds in my mind, I know that it is nothing but a flash of fantasy. Of course I cannot take him. Maybe if I didn't have my senses about me; in my current emotional state, it could have gone either way. I would never risk him or my friends, or the work we have done in that way, so I put Rocky back in his kennel and kneel at the door.

He sticks his nose through the wire and I kiss it. Kneeling, clutching the wire crate, nose to nose with my gorgeous Rottweiler, I weep. I whisper that I love him and will think of him always. I stand to leave and take one final look, choking back tears. I will never forget him and will always wonder where he went and if he is well.

I take the long way around, my eyes filled with tears, and again pass the snarling brown dog I'd tried so hard to befriend earlier. He still cowers in the back of his crate, which is again full of urine. The poor little guy is so full of fear he snarls at anyone who comes close. I walk to his crate and angrily pull the yellow caution tape off.

"Tag him, he's coming with me," I snap, impulsively. The startled barn leader looks up, unsure whether to challenge me. I'm sure I must be a sight with angry eyes, swollen from crying, and a runny nose.

"Excuse me?" he asks.

"I said tag him and take him to Outtake—Aspen Animal Shelter —he's coming with me!"

I turn and walk away. Anger overtakes my grief as it becomes a reality that Rocky will be left behind. Left for whom and to go where? These are questions for which no one will have an acceptable answer. The still snarling brown dog will take his place in our rescues, but never in my heart.

The barn leader decides it isn't worth arguing with me. He loads the brown dog's crate onto a dolly and heads for the Outtake area. Beyond that lies the dog's trip to freedom, wherever that will be.

Bland waves as she sees me walking back toward the group. I can tell by her face she is relieved that I have returned, but she still feels badly for me. She's just about to walk over and hug me when she catches sight of the dolly with the brown dog being rolled up behind me.

"Oh, crap . . . ," she mutters under her breath to Melinda. ". . . not him! We'll never get him past those military vets in Outtake. They'll want to euthanize him."

Despite her concern, Bland greets me warmly. "Are you okay? I feel so terrible about Rocky. I tried everything but they won't let him go."

I had no idea at the time, but Bland had gone as high up the chain of command as she could in an effort to get Rocky released. She had even tried to appeal to Edward, but discovered he had left to attend a meeting with governors from the Gulf Coast states hit hard by Katrina.

I smile at her. "Thank you, I know you did." The tears start flowing again. "I shouldn't have gotten so attached to him, I broke my own cardinal rule." I try to laugh through my tears, at the irony of it. "I brought him as a replacement."

I nod toward the brown dog, who now looks even more confused and frightened.

"Yes, I saw you did." Bland gives me the look she only flashes when acknowledging that I'm probably not doing the smartest thing. But she is a true friend and her support is steadfast. "I hope we can get him past them."

She motions over to a group of harried-looking techs milling about. "They're ordering that any dog who even snaps while being checked be pulled and euthanized."

"Let them try!" I've lost all patience with the mounting bureaucracy and the rush to judge these frightened animals. In the course of two days, the place has gone from complete chaos to martial law. I don't know which was better—only that I'm fed up with it all. There isn't time to know these dogs; they're being presented in their worst, most frightened, disoriented state. Some will appear more aggressive than they actually are. But in this moment of utter irrationality, the risk of challenging authority, even military authority, is of no concern to me. I'm ready to fight if I have to.

The Outtake area consists of a series of tents that surround cluttered desks manned by a few flustered workers. There are more National Guard soldiers, vets and vet techs scurry around in scrubs, carrying syringes, their stethoscopes swinging and bouncing off their chests with each step they take. They busily rush from one open tent flap into another. Dog crates are stacked and scattered everywhere, some empty, some occupied. Three harried girls handling the recordkeeping sit at tables stacked high with folders and paperwork. Loose papers are strewn over every available inch of table space in a most disorganized manner.

We aren't allowed to enter the tents to help calm our dogs. We can only sit and stare at the tent flaps, which occasionally flutter as a light breeze finds its way through the crevices and canvas. The four of us sit in silence, worried that one or two or more of the dogs will not make it out of the tents alive. Rumors swirl that the vets are fairly harsh in their decision-making.

The wait continues and, unable to sit any longer, we begin to pace. Our pacing eventually slows to a tense standstill and we're quiet but apprehensive. Melinda is concerned that the little Pomeranian with the big attitude will be pulled from the group. Jan is afraid they will pull Daisy. I stand with them, nerves frayed, needing to unleash some of the pent-up resentment that consumes me. Energy charges through me and bounces off every nerve ending, searching for a way to break out of my body. It's unnerving.

I turn and see the concern on the faces of Melinda and Jan. They have reason to worry. We're all worried, knowing that at any moment any one of these dogs that we have already come to cherish could be given an injection and silently die, there in a dim lit tent, alone.

One of the vet techs finally approaches Bland. "Are your vehicles all lined up at the gate? We can't finalize the process and release these dogs until the vehicles are here. We're required to inspect the mode in which the animals will be transported."

Bland momentarily panics as she realizes Vic still hasn't arrived with the third vehicle. She tries to bluff her way out of the situation by nodding and motioning to our two SUVs parked just outside the gate.

The vet tech peers over the top rim of her glasses. "You're planning on putting all thirteen dogs into those two SUVs? And where will the four of you sit?"

Bland looks at her and tries to decipher whether the glint in the tech's eyes is one of humor or power. Regardless, the fact that we have only two SUVs for thirteen dogs is not going to fly with the tech.

Eyes pleading, Bland quickly explains that Vic is two minutes away and will surely be at the gate before we finish processing the dogs. The girl shuffles through the paperwork she's holding and gives an exasperated look to her co-worker. We're left to interpret her look as we will.

We're trying to decide what the tech's non-response means when a tall blonde girl in a navy t-shirt walks over. She has a kind, pretty face with soft blue eyes and smiles as she approaches Bland. I can't hear what they're saying but assume it has something to do with our vehicle situation. She gently nods as Bland speaks, gives her a sympathetic look and shakes her head "no." She looks at her watch, whispers something to Bland and walks back into one of the tents. We look at Bland, who just shrugs.

Within minutes one, two, then four of our dogs are rolled out and over to the harried vet tech. We're excited but continue to hold our breath, realizing the three most questionable have yet to appear. Suddenly, Jan lets out a muffled squeal of delight as she sees Daisy's crate being rolled out. She rushes over to her and Daisy vigorously wags her tail, excited. Six crates, then seven . . . and then the little Pomeranian with the big attitude. Melinda hurries over to him. The snarling brown dog still has not emerged from the tents. My anxiety gets the better of me and my eyes fill with tears, knowing what is inevitable. My stomach is in my throat as the ninth then the tenth crates join the crowd around the checkout tables.

The nice blond girl in the navy tee walks out again and pulls Bland aside. My whole body feels weak as my nerves attack my stomach, and I feel I could vomit in the midst of all this activity. I cannot hear what she is telling Bland; I'm not sure I want to know. One of the girls at the table yells something to Bland about vehicles, but I hear nothing. I am zeroed in, eyes glued to Bland and the blonde girl. I am acutely aware of the empty gray space next to the tent flap, behind them.

Nothing. No activity. Vacant space. It is far too quiet. It can't be good.

People pass by and say things to me. I smile and nod, blankly acknowledging them but not comprehending what they say. I can't. I continue to stare at the tent flap, rippling in the wind. I memorize every crease in the dingy, yellowed canvas, the gray metal washers along the heavily-stitched tent bottom and below that the grains of sand and gravel on the asphalt. I am aware of nothing right now but that flap and the huge, empty dark hole behind it.

The toe of a dirty tennis shoe draped in green scrubs suddenly appears just inside the tent flap. A vet tech comes into view but then stops and solemnly studies the paperwork he holds. I want to walk over to him, but I'm afraid that if I stand my knees might buckle and I will fall, face first, onto the dirty concrete at our feet. The humorous thought breaks a bit of my tension, but when I chuckle at the thought, it sounds more like a grimace than a quiet giggle.

I watch as a wheel appears behind his shoe and then the glint of chrome and the squeak of a cart being rolled out. I open my mouth and try to draw in a huge breath but am momentarily paralyzed by what I see. On the cart is a crate. Inside the crate is the snarling brown dog. Alive! He remains very still at first but suddenly his head turns and one beautiful but fearful brown eye peaks out at me. Tears of joy, finally tears of joy and not sadness, flood my eyes. I brush my arm across my nose as it runs and drips onto the front of my shirt. Relief replaces anxiety. He made it! The snarling brown dog has made it out alive! I hurry over to him and he welcomes me with a snarl and pushes himself as far back in the crate as he can. I'm just about to open the crate to try to coax him when we hear Vic's Jeep screech to a halt at the gate. The warm and fuzzy greeting will have to wait.

It's all a blur of action: Paperwork signed, dogs in crates loaded into our vehicles, saying our good-byes to the medical staff. We move fast as though we're escaping, our motivation finally having the dogs to ourselves, free to give them the walks, food and love of which they are so deserving. In my euphoria, I grab the vet tech who brought the brown dog out and hug him hard, as I do the pretty blonde. I never learned their names, but I will never forget them.

I rush to the car and catch a quick glimpse of the military vet I had doubted. I am overcome with remorse, understanding and compassion. I was so sure he would decide to kill the fearful and snarling brown dog. The vet made sure the dog made it out the other side alive, and I know that could not have been easy. He catches my eye briefly and pulls his lips into a satisfied smile as he nods his head. I can't help but turn around, rush over to him and hug him.

He understands the big picture. I'm beginning to see it, too: We're all warriors in this horrible war, but we're fighting for the same thing. Together. We aren't enemies out to inflict emotional pain or hurt one another. We're on the same side, and that is the side of doing good for these animals as we combat forces beyond anyone's control. Some have tougher decisions and jobs than others. I might think being in the trenches is hard and emotional, but these vets that have to make and carry out the life and death decisions bear a far heavier burden. They care and love and grieve just as much as we do. All of us, the entire group at the Lamar Dixon facility and all the makeshift facilities, are here because we volunteered. We want to help and save as many animals as we can.

Nobody wants an animal to die. It just has to happen sometimes.

I pull away from the vet and look him in the eye. We say nothing. I smile, nod my head in respect and gratitude and walk to the car to join everyone. The three vehicles pull out of the facility. Six people and thirteen dogs sit inside, all in a much different place than when we first pulled in days ago.

We persevered. We grew. We saw terrible tragedies and joyous triumphs. We laughed and cried and cursed and perspired more than we ever believed we could. Our hearts opened and broke over and over again, multiple times a day. For that, our hearts are fuller now than ever. We hated what we witnessed, but we would never have chosen any other place to be. We experienced and survived one of the most profound crises in our nation's history.

We are just four girls from Colorado, doing what we can.

Chapter 11

WE ARRIVE AT DEB AND Vic's house and unload the crates into their garage. Before we retreat to the house, we set up fans on all the crates. We feed, water and walk all the dogs . . . . except one. The snarling brown dog refuses to eat or let me or anyone else get anywhere near him. I open his kennel and quickly shove a food bowl and some water inside as he again pushes himself against the back of the crate, baring his teeth, snarling and growling at me.

As the sun sets, we finally make it into the house and prepare for our last night in Louisiana. We take long, hot showers, put on our cutest clothes and uncork several bottles of wine. Vic is in the kitchen, cooking. A wonderfully warm, spicy smell wafts through the house. We spend a bittersweet but glorious evening drinking too much wine, eating red beans, rice and cornbread and sharing stories of our separate lives and how we all came together. We roar with laughter at photos and stories Deb and Vic tell of their past reign as Mardi Gras king and queen. We laugh and cry as we talk about the beautiful and painful experiences we have shared. It is the first time in our long, arduous adventure that we feel relaxed and open enough to feel the true spirit of New Orleans. With a tinge of sadness, I realize I never knew the city as it was. It may never be like that again.

It seems I have just drifted to sleep when Vic knocks on my door. It's four o'clock in the morning; time to get up. I take a deep breath as I think about the day ahead. Only two people and an as yet unde-termined number of the dogs will fit on the Cessna. I have volun-teered to drive back to Aspen with whatever dogs remain. Melinda begrudgingly but by necessity has agreed to drive with me, although she makes it abundantly clear that she is not a fan of road trips.

The thought of all we need to do and my desire to see the snarl-ing brown dog energizes me. I get up quickly. Dressed in shorts, a tank top, cardigan and sandals, I grab the coffee Vic offers me as I pass him in the kitchen to join Melinda, already in the garage. I head straight to the brown dog's kennel. Opening the door, I find him in his usual position, huddled against the back of the crate, teeth bared and snarling. Only this time, he sits in a pool of urine. I grab a leash, determined to lasso him and force him out of the crate. He dodges every effort I make until I eventually give up, exasperated. It is far too early in what will be a busy day to get frus-trated by this dog. "Fine, sit in it!" I bark at him, knowing I won't let him sit there long.

As I walk away from his crate, I trip on the garden hose. A smile creeps across my face as I bend to move it. I pick up the hose, turn on the water and start to gently spray inside the crate. As he sits there, I continue to increase the pressure of the spray knowing, eventually, he will run into the awaiting looped leash. I continue with the rinsing until the water runs clear. The brown dog has not budged from the back of the crate and now stares at me angrily.

Huh! I stare back at him, perplexed but impressed by his strong will. I offer him food, which he refuses, and water, which he ignores. I close his crate and silently wonder if I have made a huge mistake in rescuing him. Given his less than pleasant disposition, I'm not sure we'll be able to find a responsible home for him.

Everyone joins Melinda and me; the garage is a bevy of activity. Puppies poop everywhere. Jan, Bland and Deb walk a few of the older dogs in the darkness of the chilly, early morning. A few min-utes later we tearfully hug Deb good-bye as Vic loads twelve dog crates, our luggage and bags of miscellaneous paraphernalia into the vehicles.

We're on the road before five o'clock.

The ride to Louisiana State University is quiet as we caravan along in three SUV's. Vic is leading, followed by Jan and Bland, and then Melinda and me. Melinda is uncharacteristically quiet, asking only pertinent questions, to which I give one- or two- word responses. I am not a morning person.

We arrive at LSU. Bland and Jan walk inside to pick up the remaining five dogs. Much to my chagrin, Melinda decides to take the Pomeranian, "Cujo," out of his crate for a quick walk. Two National Guard soldiers guard the front doors of the auditorium and we strike up a conversation. I silently chuckle, waiting for the moment when one of them will bend to pet little Cujo only to be bitten by him. I watch in astonishment as one of the guys bends down, picks up Cujo and the dog sweetly curls up in his arms, moving only to lift his head to cover the guy's face in doggie kisses.

Melinda and I stare at each other, mouths agape. "You drugged him, didn't you?" I jokingly accuse her.

She laughs. "One would think. So bizarre."

In the midst of Cujo and the guard's love fest, Bland pops her head out the door, appearing upset. "Ugh. What now?"

I pass Melinda, who ignores me, temporarily infatuated with Cujo's submissive behavior. It turns out LSU will not release any cats to us, only the five dogs. We chat and quickly realize it's probably a blessing in disguise, so we willingly accept their decision and quickly load up the additional five dogs. Traffic is just beginning to build as we head for the airport, the three vehicles now jam-packed with five humans and eighteen dogs.

Steve meets us at the airport when we arrive, having flown in that morning. Our next challenge: to load as many dogs onto the plane as possible. Melinda and I are hoping to have only four or five dogs with us on our road trip to Aspen. We unload everything from all three vehicles and start to prioritize which dogs must go on the plane. Daisy, of course, has to ride with Jan, her new mom. The three puppies will fly, as we feel they're too young to endure a long road trip. Next, we load up the old black Lab to which Bland seems to be growing attached, as well as a smaller crate that is picked because it fits into a small area.

Steve walks over to where we stand and tells us he might be able to fit three more.

"What?" I turn to look at the twelve remaining crates. "Three more? Seriously? Is that all?" I'm slightly panicked.

He nods, grabs another smaller crate and heads back over to the plane. Melinda and I stare at one another yet again. A small plane taxis by and I see the pilot look over at us as he points us out to his co-pilot. Both laugh. We are a mess. It must be quite a sight on the tarmac: three SUV's with all doors and tailgates open wide; ten or so bags of luggage; coolers; dog crates; food and assorted paraphernalia strewn everywhere. In the midst of it all stand four slightly bewildered-looking women.

I walk over to the plane. My mission: to fit more dogs onto it. As it is, there are puppy crates in the plane's bathroom. Daisy is strapped into the seat next to Jan, and the old Lab sits in a crate behind the co-pilot seat, where Steve has removed a seat. It is an amusing sight, but we're not laughing as we realize that Melinda and I will be driving the long road to Aspen with nine fairly large dogs. I grimace at the thought but resign myself to putting on my best game face. I have to. I still have to break the news to Melinda. The only thing we can do is to finish this trip as fast as possible. I mentally calculate the distance. If all goes as planned, we should be in New Mexico before we stop for the night. We can make it home by early the next afternoon.

Everyone helps us load the remaining nine dogs into the two SUVs. Our precious payload includes the snarling brown dog, as well as the Irish Setter, the "sweet little furry one," the Yellow

Lab, the "black and white spotted one," the "black, furry one," the "brownish, furry, fat one," the "one we always forget" and, to my dismay, Cujo, the devil-dog.

Within minutes, we're ready to bid farewell to Bland, Jan, Steve and the nine dogs they're taking. They will probably arrive in Aspen before Melinda and I pass through Houston. Bland and Jan wave gleefully as the plane taxis and takes-off. We wave back, standing there like two women suddenly and appallingly abandoned.

"This is so not fair!" I laugh, trying to lighten up the moment. Melinda says nothing and I'm not sure if it's because she has nothing to say, or is speechless about the predicament in which she now finds herself.

We hug Vic goodbye, thank him for his and Deb's incredible hospitality, and hit the road. Neither Melinda nor I know exactly which dogs we have, only that Melinda definitely has Cujo and I definitely have the snarling brown dog. After a quick stop for gas, coffee and snacks, we pull onto I-10 and the thick morning rush hour traffic.

I'm already tired. The day has barely begun.

We leave the outskirts of Baton Rouge and traffic is still heavy. Trucks and tractor-trailers travel in both directions, ferrying supplies into and out of the hurricane-ravaged area. Traveling along the highway, I pass carload after carload of evacuees with cars filled to the brim with whatever they salvaged before fleeing their homes. Their faces look shell-shocked as they drive west, away from the physical and emotional devastation they have endured. I wonder where they're heading, grateful that I have a home and life awaiting me. Most of these people probably have nothing.

I turn on the radio and settle in for the drive, letting out a long, heavy sigh. I realize this is the first time in ten days that I've been alone. I finally have time to reflect on everything that we have experienced, as a group, as individuals. What a surreal trip! Too much to mentally process; I couldn't yet begin to do so. As hard as

I try, I can't yet bring myself to fully or even partially comprehend things. I realize I'm still locked in the numbness that has been my life for the last nine months. I see things, experience things, might feel something in the moment, but then it is all gone. No emotion remains, only images of the events.

Feeling hazy from too little sleep and the brightness of the morning, I turn up the radio and zone out. I smile as The Eagles' "Ol' 55"comes on, a perfect song for the moment.

Suddenly, images of the past ten days flash through my head like a slideshow set to the song. The decision to go, the trip to New Orleans, arriving at Lamar Dixon, all the faces of the dogs and cats and horses, the people, the tents in which some slept, Liz and Deb and Vic, their homes, the laughter, the tears, the toasts. I felt alive; I wished I had stayed a little longer. As hard as it was to be there, it was sad to leave and to wonder about all the dogs still alone on the streets and in the makeshift shelters. Many groups cared for the people of New Orleans—that was a given—but it was so heartwarming to see the many groups, large and small, that came together for the animals. Everyone from the nation's largest animal welfare organizations to individuals like the four of us had converged on the area. I will miss it and I do now wish I could have stayed a little longer.

I drift back to the melody of the song and realize that, one way or another, everything is going to be alright. For New Orleans and for me. What a journey we've taken. To come together, both damaged and needy, and to part both stronger and more determined to survive.

We cross into Texas and decide to make a brief stop for gas and to let the dogs out, as some of them have been in their kennels since 5 a.m. We quickly realize this is the first time we've had to deal with all nine of them at once, and aren't quite sure how to coordinate things. We decide to take the dogs out of their crates, one at a time, and tie them to whatever we can find. We discover a spot in a grassy area behind the building where there are a couple trees, a couple signposts and a fence.

The first kennel contains the snarling brown dog. I'm not in the mood for his attitude right now, but know I won't give up on him. I open the door expecting him to be in his usual state—crouched back, teeth-bared, snarling at me. I'm taken by complete surprise as he greets me happily, tail wagging, eyes shining and seemingly smiling. I stand back and look at him and realize that maybe, just maybe, we have crossed a bridge and are now friends. I smile back at him and am overcome with happiness as I realize he must finally feel safe with me. He's ready to trust. I speak gently to him and when I see that he's comfortable, give him a quick hug and take him out of his crate and into the sunshine for the first time in a long time. It is a joyous moment but short-lived. There are four other dogs waiting for me to let them out.

Moments later, all the dogs are out of their crates and securely tied up, enjoying the sunshine, grass and fresh water. Melinda and I stand back and look at our furry charges. There before us, bound to a fence, trees and poles, nine dogs turn and stare back. We take them all in. We're not quite sure what to do next, and the dogs aren't quite sure who we are or what we expect from them.

"Sit!" I command, just for the fun of it. Of the six or so standing, three of them immediately sit. "Well, that's not bad, is it? Should we test them and see how many will shake?"

Melinda and I discuss whether we should walk each one individually so they have some one-on-one time with us, but decide against it. We keep them safely tethered and give them bowls of water and treats. When we realize they probably won't pee where they're leashed, we decide to take each one on a quick walk before loading them back into the car and hitting the road.

We finally reach Houston around 2 p.m., already a bit behind schedule. We weave our way through the city until we locate the van rental office, pull in and park just out of view. We're unsure whether animals are allowed in cargo vans, and we don't want to get busted, so we haven't confessed to the rental agency that we're transporting dogs. We don't want any complications. Melinda and I feel like criminals as we work to maneuver the two dog-filled vehicles into parking spaces undetected by the rental car agents. One major concern is that it's blazing hot outside and we don't want to leave any of the dogs in a parked vehicle, even for a short while. Even in the shade, it will be stifling in their kennels within minutes. We park as close as we can but still out of sight of the office, and Melinda rushes in to rent the van.

A few minutes later, she comes out of the building looking extremely exasperated.

"What's up?" I ask.

"The cargo van is not a cargo van, it's a mini-van and it's the only van they have!" She's clearly and understandably frustrated. "What are we going to do?"

I sit in dumbfounded silence for a moment. "What can we do?" I turn and stare into the distance. I'm usually in better control of situations, but I'm at a complete loss with this one. I had called everywhere before we left Louisiana and this was the only "cargo" van I could find.

Now I know why.

I turn to Melinda. "Do you think we can fit everyone and everything in the mini-van?"

I'm desperate. We have to get these dogs and ourselves home to Colorado as soon as possible. There's something even more urgent: getting back to the dogs that are sitting in the vehicle behind the building. We have to figure out something—fast.

"There's no way!" Melinda's frustration grows. I can't blame her. "We're not going to fit all the crates and crap from two SUV's into one mini-van. Are you serious?"

As the realization that it's the only available solution dawns on me, I look up at her. "Yes, probably. We're just going to have to take all the dogs out of their crates and hope that they get along with each other!"

Melinda looks at me as if I have lost my mind. Maybe I have. "I can't believe you're even thinking about letting all those dogs loose together in the mini-van. That's crazy! What if they start fighting? This is unbelievable!"

She stares into the distance and looks like she's going to cry. I've never seen her like this; she's usually strong and stoic. Now, as beads of sweat form on her forehead and start to slowly trickle down her face, she looks so lost and helpless. I'm touched by her vulnerability and it makes me feel closer to her in that moment than ever. We are in this together and will survive it, together.

I start to panic. "Look, it's hot. We have to get back to the dogs. Just go back in, rent it and we'll figure it out. We have no choice. If it doesn't work we'll return it and figure out a Plan B."

We stare at each other as we think it through. We know our options are few, if we have any at all. Especially right here, right now. With its close proximity to New Orleans, Houston is absorbing the brunt of the influx of evacuees and response teams. We know our options are as limited as our resources. We must find a way to fit all nine dogs into the minivan and make it work. Not to mention nine crates, our luggage, supplies, dog paraphernalia and ourselves. It will be a daunting task, to put it mildly.

After renting the minivan, we start to consolidate the contents of the two SUVs into the one vehicle and return them. We find a fenced-in parking lot close to where we will return the vehicles, and ferry back and forth until we have all three vehicles parked close to the tiniest but only sliver of grass we can find in front of the fence. One by one, we take the dogs out of the crates, tie them to a fence and give them a bowl of water.

Melinda continues to pamper Cujo; why, I don't know. The dog is so mean I am sure it could fend off a Pit Bull if put up against one. Instead of tying Cujo to the fence with the other dogs, she keeps him with her as she works. It makes the unpacking and packing a bit more complicated as she drags him around and he slows her down. I become agitated as I watch her. At one point, needing both hands, she places Cujo's leash in her mouth and forages in the car. She catches my eye and I give her a look of disapproval, but say nothing.

It's a challenge as we arrange and rearrange bags and boxes and try to fit everything in the minivan as compactly as possible. I'm busying myself in the front of the van, seeing that anything I might need on the trip is within reach from the driver's seat. Melinda is somewhere else either working or with Cujo. It's blazing hot and I'm soaked with perspiration, as I'm sure she is. Our frustrations are high and our tempers short and rising. I feel like I'm carrying the brunt of work while she plays and babies Cujo. She probably feels that I'm being pushy and uncaring. I just want to get the job done as fast as possible so we can get back on the road. Precious traveling time is slipping away with every minute we spend here messing around. The dogs are hot and I want to get them into the air-conditioned van as fast as possible. After finishing up front, I decide to tackle the large pile of dog paraphernalia at the rear of the van. I sort through the bags and, without looking or even thinking, reach and open the back of the van to start loading. The large hatched door pops open and rises quickly.

"Anne!"

"What?" Melinda startles me. I'm angry and hot. My clothes are so soaked they stick to me. I whirl around with the intention of yelling back at her for the way she has just screamed at me. I stop in my tracks, stare in disbelief and open my mouth wide, but say nothing. Unbeknownst to me, Melinda had tied Cujo's leash to the wiper blade on the back window of the hatch door. When I popped open the hatch, Cujo had immediately been yanked off his feet and swiftly thrust skyward. He now hangs in mid-air, suspended from the wiper blade on the open hatch. The leash still around his neck, he is twirling in little circles, like a Cirque du Soleil acrobat.

"Oh, crap!" I cry out, panicked. I quickly slam the hatch closed and Cujo slumps to the ground in a cloud of dust, coughing and gasping.

Distressed, I turn to Melinda. "Oh, my God, I'm so sorry. Why didn't you tell me you tied him to the window?"

Melinda can't contain herself. Cujo is obviously fine and we both fall over in fits of hysterical laughter. We laugh so hard tears roll down our beet red cheeks. I'm sure I'm going to wet my pants.

Out of nowhere, a man's voice: "I saw that!"

We both look up, startled. The driver of a courtesy shuttle has stopped in the road. For a split second we freeze, staring at one another with guilty faces as if we have just been caught committing a crime. The man bursts out laughing. Relieved, Melinda and I laugh even harder, now that we have been caught doing something so incredibly stupid. Cujo, fully recovered, is not at all fazed by what happened. He joins in our merriment, prancing around, his eyes dancing and bushy tail wagging happily, as if he knows he's the star.

The shuttle driver leaves and we continue to load everything until all that remains are the nine plastic crates and nine dogs. Four of the crates are extremely large, four are medium in size and the last is the small crate in which Cujo travels.

"What are we going to do with them?" Melinda nods towards the crates. I stare at the stack for a moment.

"Break them down and put them on top of the van?" I ask, trying to convince myself. I have no idea what to do with them, but we can't leave them here. Besides, we might need them when we stop for the night.

Melinda rolls her eyes and we start breaking the crates down into two pieces each, putting the halves one inside the other. The completed stack is almost five feet high. We stand back, look at the stack, survey the roof and return to the stack. I remind myself that I'm in the midst of my initial breast reconstruction phase. Tubes are implanted under my skin and run down both sides of my torso, connecting my implants to little ports that are located midway between my armpit and hip. The tubes prohibit me from extending my arms over my head, especially if I'm holding any weight at all.

It quickly becomes apparent we will need help. The dogs' panting and the blistering heat add a sense of urgency to our task. "Where's the damn shuttle driver when you need him?" I ask, discouraged.

My eyes pan the wide sea of cars, concrete and asphalt. I stop when I see a figure at the opposite end of the parking lot walking toward us, smoking a cigarette. "There's a guy coming this way, maybe he'll help us." I nod toward the approaching figure.

Melinda squints. "Is it a guy? That's not a guy!" She squints harder, trying to make out the gender as the person draws closer.

"No, I think it's a guy, look at the size of his arms." I reply.

"I don't know, look at the hair, it's really long and silky. I think she's a girl. We can't ask a girl to help us put the crates up there."

Melinda looks at me, clearly annoyed.

The figure walks closer, but we still can't determine if it is a guy or a girl. Desperation grows as the dogs' panting becomes more labored. I give them all fresh water, pouring some down each of their necks and backs. We have to get them out of the heat. I don't care what it will take.

I call out to the figure, now within earshot. "Excuse me! Hello! Excuse me . . ." I wave. "Hi, yes . . . can we ask a favor?" I hate looking so girly and helpless.

We get the attention of the person, who turns and slowly walks toward us. The closer they get, the more uncertain we are if it is a man or woman.

"I feel terrible, but I still can't tell! I know this is rude but look at the boobs, do they look like man boobs or woman boobs?" I whisper to Melinda, panic mounting.

"I don't know. They look like small girl boobs, but they could be small man boobs." She giggles.

It is such a strange predicament to be in, knowing we will quickly be face-to-face with an androgynous person. I have no clue about the correct protocol. The person is short and stocky, olive-skinned, probably Hispanic but possibly Indian with long, straight, dark hair. It's unfortunate the person's eyes are hidden behind sunglasses, because seeing their eyes would help us figure this out. The clothing doesn't help, either: blue jeans, unisex boots and a dark t-shirt. I'm distracted, fascinated at not being able to determine this person's sex. I stare, mesmerized. I look at the hands, hopeful they will reveal the gender or at least a clue, but at this distance, they look pudgy, generic and nondescript with no rings.

"It's Pat!" I whisper out of their earshot, making reference to the androgynous Saturday Night Live character whose name further blurred the line of sexual identity.

Melinda laughs. "It is! It's Pat!"

We compose ourselves as "Pat" reaches us. Regardless of which sex Pat is, we need help as we explain our predicament. Pat is kind and more than willing to help. Taking command of the situation, Pat tells Melinda that if she gets up on the roof of the van, Pat will hand the heavy crate halves up to her one at a time.

We still don't know if we're talking to a man or a woman. We explain how we came to be in the situation. Pat smiles in amusement at the dogs tied to the nearby fence, panting but waiting patiently. S/he helps Melinda secure the crates with bungee cords and then, without much conversation, put hands in pockets, wishes us well and walks off. Melinda and I silently watch as Pat walks into the distance. We're touched and humbled at the kindness we were afforded . . . but still as dumbfounded as we were when Pat walked up. "Well, that was different," Melinda says before laughing.

I can only smile in wonderment at the encounter with this stranger. The person appeared when needed, quickly and quietly helped us and then left, all within minutes. I look up into the bright blue, cloudless sky and offer a smile of gratitude.

We load the dogs and realize it is good that they had to sit close to one another along the fence. It gave them an opportunity to become familiar with each other before being tossed into the van together. Surprisingly, once inside the minivan, they all get along and seem to maintain their good temperaments despite the close quarters. I wonder if it has anything to do with the turmoil they have been through. To finally ride, loose in a car like they probably rode pre-Katrina, is more than likely the first sense of normalcy they've had in over two weeks.

However, we're still apprehensive. We watch them intently, hoping we can keep them calm for the entire trip. We organize how we will seat each dog, and then quickly place them in their assigned spots. The three larger dogs—the Irish Setter, Yellow Lab and Brown Dog, the snarling one—go into the seat furthest back. The five medium-sized dogs fit compactly on the middle seat and entire floor area.

For a split second, we smile at our accomplishment. Then we close the doors to begin our journey. Within seconds, they have all jumped out of their seats and most squish together behind the front seats, trying to get to Melinda and me. All except the Irish Setter, who sits regally in her assigned spot. I look at her and, meeting her eyes, sense sadness about her. I can't get to her to pet and assure her that all will be well. I silently promise that we will do all we can to find her people.

The floor of the van transforms into an intricate carpet woven of colored and textured dog fur, noses and tails. There's a lot of butt-sniffing and a couple low growls as the dogs work out the hierarchy. The Brown, Furry Fat dog immediately jumps into the front seat and then onto the floor of the passenger seat. Melinda looks at me helplessly and then gently nudges the dog to try and move her into the back. The dog is dead weight, curled up and refusing to budge.

"Just leave her there, I'll use her as a footrest," Melinda says.

We look at her feet. It looks as if she's wearing big dog slippers. "Looks warm and comfy," I laugh, turning on the car and blasting the air conditioner. We sit for a minute and savor the cool air blowing on us. Melinda still holds Cujo, who now starts growling fiercely at the other dogs.

"Melinda. That dog is not riding up front with us!" I'm adamant.

"Why not?"

"Why not? Because, obviously he's already pissed off. He's still biting you and he'll get the other ones all riled up. We'll end up having a huge dogfight in this small van. I'm already worried about them all being together. That dog loose up here is like throwing a match into a gas can."

My frustration has mellowed in weariness. I'm anxious to get on the road and dread the thought of battling Houston rush hour traffic, which was heavy an hour ago. I know by now it will be bumper to bumper. I won't allow myself to think about how behind schedule we now are. It depresses me as I realize there is no way we will make up the time or reach New Mexico tonight. We might get as far as Amarillo or the Texas panhandle.

"Then what am I supposed to do with him?" she asks, a hint of hostility in her tone.

I look at her arms, covered in tiny Cujo bites and scratches. I have to smile. She is obviously very attached to the little Tasmanian Devil. In my weariness, I almost give in, but quickly get my wits about me. We're responsible for these dogs now and we can't take any chances, given they're all just getting to know one another. "Put little Cujo in his crate with a blanket and water and put him in the very back of the van on top of the luggage," I tell her.

Melinda resigns herself to the fact that I'm probably right and starts preparing his small crate. I tilt my head back and silently count to ten as more wasted minutes tick away. It doesn't help developing tensions that every time Melinda moves Cujo, he emotes a ferocious growl that sounds more like a Rottweiler than a cute little lap dog. I get out of the car and help Melinda tuck him amongst the luggage.

We both step back and look at the fully loaded van with crates stacked high on the roof and eight little doggie faces staring back at us. It's quite a sight. "We look like the freakin' Griswold family on our way to Wally World!" I laugh. "Do you think those crates will interfere with the aerodynamics of the van?"

I only then remember we still have to return the two SUVs to the rental agency a few blocks away. It isn't within walking distance, especially given the heat, so we'll have to make two trips, taking one SUV at a time. In the heavy traffic, it takes almost an hour. It's now almost six o'clock and we're just getting onto the interstate. We no sooner make our way up the entrance ramp than we see a Starbucks. We pull off. Caffeine is a necessity, given the long drive ahead of us.

As we sit in the parked car, sipping the delicious coffee beverages, we turn and look behind us. Eight dogs fill the seats, every inch of available floor space covered, and happily stare back at us. The ninth dog continues to growl at nothing, but is safely confined to his crate. They're a motley crew, extremely lovable and, so far, well-mannered with one another, especially given what they have been through today alone. Melinda and I smile warmly at them. It feels good, knowing we have saved them from the nightmare they were living. We finish our coffee, pull out onto the highway and head north. I still hope to make it to the Texas panhandle.

The Friday evening traffic is backed up as far as the eye can see. It takes almost an hour to reach the outskirts of Houston. The setting sun blazes through the windows, making it seem even hotter than it actually is. We roll down the windows for a brief respite from the circulating air, which has been made unpleasant by nine furry, panting and gassy dogs.

"Are we still in Texas?" Melinda laughs. "I feel like we've been here all day!"

It's eight o'clock before we're finally free of Houston, the great urban jungle. The dogs are quiet, except for Brown Dog. In an effort to get as close to me as possible, he has managed to wedge himself between my driver's seat and the thick door jamb. Now he's stuck, panting in my ear and drooling on my shoulder. I've had enough of his slobbering and hot breath on my already over-heated neck, so I try to push him into the back seat. He pushes right back and wedges himself tighter into the small crevice. Once again, he's showing signs of stubbornness.

When I turn to reprimand him, he gives me the sweetest, most endearing look. He just wants to be close to me. My heart melts. What a difference a day has made in his demeanor! Reminding myself that he hasn't felt a kind, human touch he totally trusted in over ten days, I let him stay where he is. I'm already filthy, so a little extra drool is no big deal.

I let out a deep breath and start to relax back into road warrior groove. Finally! Back on the road and headed home.

Melinda finishes the cell phone calls she has been making non-stop since we got on the road. "Can we stop at the next exit? I need to pee."

Frustrated at the thought of having to stop, yet again, and afraid of what I will say if I open my mouth, I say nothing. I stare straight ahead, finding escape in the calmness of my zombie-like state. I want to get some miles behind us fast. I hadn't anticipated stop-ping again until our gas tank was empty. We couldn't have been more mismatched travelers.

"Did you hear me?" Melinda asks.

"Yes." I nod my head and silently fall back onto my years of meditation to get me through the moment. I remind myself of how bad stress is for my still healing body. I take a deep breath, slowly let it out and try to calm my complaining mind by reminding myself to find the good in the moment. If nothing else, I'm alive. I've helped to rescue eighteen dogs from a hell they barely survived. The thoughts put me in a better mood, and I decide we'll make the best of it by taking the opportunity to feed the dogs and let them stretch their legs.

We pass a highway sign that gives the distance to Dallas. I mentally calculate how long it will take us to get there, and realize we'll now be lucky to make Dallas before stopping for the night. That means another long day of driving tomorrow. Tears fill my eyes and slowly roll down my cheeks. I try to stifle them. I have shed more tears in the last ten days than I have in the last few years. They have to stop.

We exit at a small town that reminds me of a 60's sitcom. We pass quaint clapboard homes, a church and, typical to all small Texas towns, a Dairy Queen. It's Friday night, Texas high school football night, and the place is hopping. Finding a deserted park down a dark, tree-lined street, we stop and start to unload the dogs, one by one. I try to get Brown, Furry Fat dog off the floor of the car, but she steadfastly refuses to budge. The dog hasn't moved since claiming her spot in Houston. We check her breathing and gum color to make sure she isn't sick and, confident that she isn't, decide she has a thyroid problem, is extremely laid back or simply does not want to give up her safe haven. Being the ever-faithful dog servant that I am, I take her a bowl of food, but she turns away from it. I offer a bowl of water, and am satisfied when she willingly laps at it, all the while watching me suspiciously.

Melinda has taken Cujo out of his crate and lets him run loose. He struts around like the cock of the walk in front of the tied-up dogs, taunting them with his leash-free independence. I watch him, knowing it's just a matter of time before he gets too close to one of them and they nail him. If that happenes, at his size, it will be a problem.

"Melinda, leash Cujo up."

"Why? He's so cute. I feel sorry for him."

"He's not 'so cute'—he's Satan in fur! Leash him up now before one of the other dogs bites him. Please. I couldn't deal with that happening right now."

I'm on the brink of more tears and frustrated about it. We should have been almost to New Mexico by now.

Obligingly, Melinda scoops up Cujo, who proceeds to bite her. She gives me a sullen look as if it is my fault. I ignore her brooding as we continue to care for the dogs. I stand back and watch them, all tied to trees. They have such different personalities. Some eat ferociously, some nibble at their food, and a couple others ignore their bowls entirely. Some sniff the area busily while others lay quietly, looking around and taking everything in. They're adorable, terribly trusting of us and behaving admirably. Now I'm glad we stopped and let them out. It's a warm evening, but a cool breeze blows through every few moments. What a stark contrast, this quiet and peaceful park, compared with their previous nights, kenneled in the restless environment at Lamar Dixon.

After fifteen minutes or so, we load them back into the van, grab a bite to eat and return to the road. The dogs curl up and sleep for the reminder of the evening, so the trip to Dallas is somewhat uneventful. Melinda continues to marvel at the fact that we're still in Texas, to which I repeatedly reply, "Yes, Melinda, it's a big state."

It's well past midnight when we roll into the Dallas area. Melinda decides that she's hungry and I offer to keep my eyes out for an open drive-thru. This doesn't sit well with her, and she insists we try to find a nice, sit-down restaurant because, after all, she has been stuck in a car since five o'clock this morning.

"I understand, Melinda, but it's almost 1 a.m. I don't think we're going to find anything. Besides, I feel really dirty and I'm covered in dog hair and drool."

I'm also exhausted, and definitely not in the mood for an evening out. Right now, all I want is a shower and a bed. I can barely keep my eyes open. They feel tired and scratchy as if the proverbial sandman has visited and dusted them. I can barely think or talk, never mind eat.

"I want to at least try to find one." She is annoyed with my lack of enthusiasm.

I feel bad for her. She is clearly out of her comfort zone on this long road trip. I don't have the energy to argue, even though I know the search will be futile. I ask that she point out any open restaurant that she sees. Big mistake. She points out two or three that "look open." Each time we exit the interstate and drive by the restaurant, we find it closed and return to the interstate. My nerves are shot, but I'm trying my hardest to be accommodating.

Once again, she points out a restaurant, and I dutifully exit. It's closed. This time, as we try to get back onto the interstate, we become completely lost in a maze of warehouses and industrial buildings. We can clearly see the interstate towering above us, but there are no entrance ramps in sight. It is now after 1 a.m. and we finally find the interstate, get back on the road and head north. I look at the clock and realize we have been up and traveling for over twenty hours. My fatigue soaks into my bones.

We blindly drive in search of a restaurant for so long that we now find ourselves in Denton, a northwest suburb of Dallas. We grab some tasteless fast food, as I had suggested an hour before, and head for a lit "Vacancy" sign in the distance. We laugh, remembering how the first night of the adventure was spent in a crappy motel. It's only fitting that the last night should be, too. This time, instead of carrying apprehension, we carry the rewards. We have nine adorable dogs—well, eight adorable dogs—and Cujo. Now we have to sneak them into one motel room. Melinda and I agree it is probably smarter for us to room together so we can be there to help one another should any situations arise.

I pull into the motel parking lot and Melinda hops out of the van. "Get a room on the ground floor," I yell to her.

A few moments later she's back in the van, key in hand, laughing. "What?"

"There were only two rooms available. The one on the lower floor is right there." She points to the room directly next to the office window, where the desk clerk sits. "Or the one I rented, which is upstairs on that corner." She points to an upstairs door on the opposite end of the building.

I nod in approval. "Good call."

We park as close to the stairs as we can. Trying to be quiet at this very late hour is difficult when unloading nine unruly dogs. Our activity has awakened them and they pace and jump around, each wanting to be first out. We know that, as soon as we open one door, eight of them will try to bolt through it at once. We discuss logistics, how to best get the nine dogs upstairs, who will take which dog and whether we will take them to the room one, two or three at a time. I can't decide if we should walk them before taking them to the room, or simply pile them into the room and then take them out in groups. It's quite a challenge traveling with nine dogs.

We cautiously open the van door, put leashes on the dogs and start taking them, as quietly as we can, up the concrete steps and into the room. We make several trips, the last to bring our luggage and Cujo, who started growling the moment we stopped the van. Exhausted, we close the hotel room door and drop the luggage to the floor. We can finally start to relax a little. The relaxation is short-lived as the dogs, sniffing everything in sight, proceed to hike their legs and start marking their territory.

"No!" I yell at them. I grab some treats in an effort to distract them.

It's cramped in the room with two Queen beds, nine dogs, Melinda, me, and our luggage. We can't move without bumping into dogs and each other. Melinda puts Cujo's crate on the low dresser. Several of the dogs jump up, sniffing it and knocking it around with their noses. Cujo flips out and lets out a long string of fierce, guttural growls. Other dogs have leaped up onto the beds, their eyes gleeful and beckoning for some playtime. I can't blame them, after being cooped up in the van for a very long day.

"No!" I repeat, somewhat disingenuously. I wish I had the energy to play. They deserve it.

Instead, worn out, I fall onto a bed. "I don't know if I can muster up the strength to take a shower. I think I'll wait and take one in the morning."

I motion to Cujo, his crate vibrating as his anxiety grows. "What are you going to do with him?" I ask.

"I don't know. Try to let him out of his crate?" Melinda bends and peers into the kennel door.

"No freaking way, Melinda!" I find it incredulous that she would even think about letting this rabid dog out.

Sulking, Melinda takes Cujo into the bathroom, where she feeds him and gives him some time out of the crate. I take the opportunity to wash up, brush my teeth, put on a fresh nightie and crawl into bed.

Several of the dogs immediately jump onto the bed to snuggle with me. I can't believe how physically tired I am. The day had started in Louisiana at 4 a.m. and it was now after 2 a.m. I chuckle. "And we're still in Texas."

My whole body aches. Vibrations of the road course through my body, and my ears start ringing. I'm suddenly overcome with the feeling that someone is watching me. I pry one eye open and jerk back, startled. Three of the dogs, including Brown Dog, are standing directly over me, staring down, their faces inches from my face. I lie motionless, afraid to move a muscle, and stare back at them. It's slightly unnerving. I don't really know these dogs and I have no idea what they're thinking. But I'm in a vulnerable position and so a bit hesitant to move. Still staring at me intently, Brown Dog opens his mouth to pant and drips of drool fall onto the sheet covering my chest. I'm too tired to care. I command them to lie down and, surprisingly, they obey.

I close my eyes. Seconds later, I hear Melinda come out of the bathroom with Cujo. He is now alternately growling and barking, and I try to ignore both he and Melinda, hoping they will think I'm asleep. Cujo's growling grows louder.

"Melinda! Shush him! He'll wake-up the people in the room next door. We can't afford to get busted with nine dogs in the room!" I whisper angrily.

"What should I do? He won't stop."

"I don't know. Put him in the bathroom and close the door."

She dutifully takes Cujo into the bathroom and leaves him in the bathtub behind the closed door. We can still hear him growling. Melinda takes the bedspread off her bed and wraps Cujo's crate, carefully ensuring there are air holes so he can breathe. We still hear his muffled growling, but it's now faint enough that we can probably get some sleep. I snuggle down deep into the covers and push one or two of the dogs out of my sleeping space. Brown Dog has curled up on the pillow next to my head, his butt facing me. I nudge him away and, as if on cue, he circles around and faces me, putting his nose into the nape of my neck. He obviously had been well loved by someone who he misses terribly. Determined to sleep, I again focus on relaxing my over-active mind. I start to drift off into a deep, heavy, luscious darkness.

"I can't sleep," Melinda whispers loudly.

I can't believe my ears. Melinda has the strangest sleep habits of anyone I know. She routinely goes to bed well after midnight and is up before six o'clock. If she happens to fall asleep before midnight, she will usually wake up around three in the morning and read or watch a movie. I don't understand how she exists on so little sleep.

"Melinda, please, I'm exhausted and need some sleep. I'm sorry if you can't sleep. I can. Good night." It is the last thing out of my mouth as I fall into a deep, comatose sleep.

I'm pulled out of the deep dark caverns of sleep by someone nudging me. I vaguely detect panic in the voice. "Oh, no. Oh, no! Anne, wake up!"

"Huh?" It's all I can get out. I'm in a totally disoriented fog and don't remember where I am or who I'm with.

"I was going to go and get something out of the car. When I opened the door some of the dogs got out!" Melinda is freaking out.

"What?" I bolt straight up.

"Some dogs got out. I was going to the car and they got out." She's almost tearful.

"Oh my God, Melinda! Go and see if you can find them!" I quickly throw back the covers and get out of bed as Melinda opens the door and peers out into the night.

"Oh, here's a couple." She pulls two of the dogs into the open door, trying not to let any others out. Fortunately, the dogs hadn't ventured far and were sitting outside the door.

I stop getting dressed and quickly perform a dog count. Two are missing. "Go and find them." I tell her, crawling back onto the bed.

She created the situation, she can fix it. I know that if she doesn't return in a minute or two, I'll definitely get up and help her. If they're close-by, then she can do whatever it takes to get them back in the room.

I doze for a moment and am again awakened. Melinda has returned, gripping the collars of the two missing dogs. "I found them!" she cries out, joyously and obviously relieved.

Those are the last words I hear before I fall into an unconscious state.

As with past mornings, the next morning comes far too soon. The alarm goes off at 6 a.m. We've had less than four hours of sleep. I hit the snooze and sleepily ask, "One more hour?" Melinda grunts her approval. It seems like five minutes later when the alarm goes off again. This time, we know we have to get up and face the long day ahead of us. Melinda jumps out of her bed and starts dressing. I pull myself up, my body aching and exhausted from the toll of the last ten days.

Immediately, the room is alive with too much activity. Dogs jump off the beds and again start hiking their legs, little squirts going everywhere.

"No!" Melinda and I both scream in unison.

"Dammit!" I let one fly. As I might have mentioned, I am not a morning person. I haven't been awake five minutes and I'm already stressing out. I grab some tissue and start soaking up the tiny wet spots. This road trip is quickly becoming a nightmare and we're only halfway home.

"We've gotta walk these guys fast," I tell Melinda, suddenly wide awake. "I'll take a few and you take some."

We take the dogs out two and three at a time, let them pee and quickly head back to the room. We need to pack and get on the road fast. It is much easier to handle the dogs when they're contained and occupied in the minivan versus running around the hotel room together.

"I can't believe we're still in Texas."

This time, I don't bother to respond to Melinda. Sunglasses on, my bag on my shoulder and two dogs leashed up and ready to go, I ask Melinda for the car key so I can start loading everyone. Melinda looks around and realizes she can't find the key. She looks through her purse, her pants, the dresser, the bathroom, the bed . . . still no keys. We start unpacking, with Melinda pulling stuff out of everything and throwing it everywhere. No keys. I'm livid. My mind goes back to the night before and it worries me to think of the many random routes Melinda may have walked in search of the dogs. The car key could be anywhere. We continue to search, now in ridiculous places like under the beds and in drawers we knew we hadn't opened.

I ask Melinda to mentally retrace her steps from the night before. Twenty minutes later, we sit on the beds facing each other, both of us ready to cry. I contemplate calling the rental agency, but we're so mentally exhausted that we can't clearly comprehend things or decide what we should do next.

At that moment Cujo, still in the bathroom, lets out a fierce growl.

"Did you have them in the bathroom when you took Cujo in there?" I ask. Melinda jumps up and runs into the bathroom.

"I found them! Got 'em!" she yells cheerfully. "They were under the blanket—I must have dropped them when I put Cujo in the tub."

Instantly relieved, we quickly repack our things. Minutes later, we open the door and scan the area like sleuths in a campy spy movie. A man stands on the balcony landing by the stairs smoking a cigarette. I start down the stairs with one bag and two dogs.

"Good morning." I nod as I quickly pass him.

"Mornin'," he replies in a deep Texas drawl.

I load the two dogs into the van as Melinda follows with two more. The man on the balcony watches as we load them. I walk upstairs and leash up two more dogs. This time as I pass the man, I just smile, nod and continue down the stairs as fast as I can, hoping he won't say anything. I try to load the two dogs into the van as the four already inside jockey to escape through the open door.

"Stay!" I screech at them, now battling six excited dogs. The man on the balcony silently watches the commotion. I motion to Melinda to bring the seventh and eighth dogs down to me. As she again passes the man, his curiosity must finally get the better of him.

"How many dogs y'all got in there?" he yells down to me, laughing.

I smile. "Only a couple more." I don't want to draw attention to what we're doing, but I think that ship has sailed.

Melinda comes down the stairs carrying Cujo's crate. She smiles at the man, who is becoming more amused with each passing dog.

"Katrina rescues," Melinda says and keeps walking.

He blows out some cigarette smoke, smiles and then calls down to us from the landing. "You ladies are doin' a good thing." He gives us the thumbs up sign and we beam.

Bags and dogs loaded, we jump in the car, stop for gas and coffee and are back on the road again by 8 a.m. I check my phone messages and hear one from our good friend, Cheryl. She heard we would be passing through Dallas and was thinking of asking her husband, Sam, if we could fly from Dallas to Aspen with them on their Gulfstream. She wants to know how many dogs we have with us, how big they are and if all their crates will fit in the interior cargo area of the jet. I chuckle as I envision the nine dog crates crammed on the jet with the four of us for the duration of the flight. Cheryl loves animals and Sam is a prince of a guy with a great sense of humor, but that might be pushing it a bit.

I continue listening to my messages. There's one from Seth, from the Aspen Animal Shelter, freaking out about eighteen dogs coming in and another from Bland warning me that Seth is freaking out. The last of my messages is from Edward, wondering how my journey is going and apologizing for not being there to see us off. He asks that I call and let him know how we're doing. This time I feel no emotion when listening to his message. Nothing is necessarily wrong with us but nothing is right either.

I turn my phone off and contemplate whether or not to tell Melinda about Cheryl's offer. At the height of one of our more trying times, Melinda had started calling private jet services to arrange for us all to be flown from Houston. I argued with her that it would cost a small fortune, but she was upset and said she didn't care how much it would cost—she was going to fly us home. When the jet service confirmed that it would cost over $20,000, she became a bit more rational and agreed to continue with the drive.

I decide to tell Melinda. It wouldn't be fair not to. "Do you think we should call her back and see if it's possible to fly to Aspen with them?" I ask. We would have to turn around and drive the hour or so back to the airport in Dallas.

"Definitely, call her," Melinda insists, desperate to end this road trip from hell.

"I don't know. Let's think about it." I don't want to turn around and backtrack. "We could almost be home by the time their jet will get us to Aspen. If we fly, we'll have to drive back to Dallas, hang out with the dogs for a few hours, unload the van, put the crates back together, load all the dogs back into their crates, return the van, load everything onto the plane and hope we haven't upset Sam with it all. And, we don't know for sure that it will even be an option once they hear how many dogs we have." Just the thought of it overwhelms me. "I think I'd rather just keep driving."

Melinda voices strong disagreement and wants to at least try to fly back with Sam and Cheryl. Call it divine intervention, but after a few moments of reflection, she agrees it's probably better not to have to deal with all the added logistics that flying with them would entail. I breathe a sigh of relief. As much as we both love them, it is just too much. We resign ourselves to the long drive.

As we drive along the empty, desolate countryside between Dallas and Wichita Falls, boredom sets in. I look in the rearview mirror and catch Brown Dog humping away on Lightly Spotted Dog. He is not neutered.

"Hey! Stop that! You! Brown Dog!" I yell.

Melinda turns and swats him. Begrudgingly, he dismounts. Brown Dog has become quite the humper and eagerly takes up with the dog nearest to him. The majority of the dogs aren't neutered, which makes any humping a crisis to be immediately averted. We don't know for sure which dogs might have been spayed, but it is very certain that Brown Dog still possesses his testicles.

We seek ways to break the ensuing boredom. We decide it will be beneficial to name the dogs. We've been referring to them as Brown Dog, Furry Dog, Lightly Spotted Dog and such, sort of like Indian names in old western movies. Brown Dog and Lightly Spotted Dog seem to like to hang together, so we decide to name Brown Dog "Jethro" and Lightly Spotted Dog "Ellie Mae." We had spilled cookies in the car and covered Brown, Furry Fat dog who was curled up at Melinda's feet with powdered sugar, so we name her "Sweetie." The Yellow Lab becomes "Lab", because, in our sheer exhaustion, we find it extremely funny. We name the beautiful red Irish Setter "Stella" because we like saying "Stellllaaaa!" The last one we name "Hedy Lamar" for no particular reason, other than we like how it sounds.

The Texas countryside becomes even more remote and lifeless. We left the interstate a couple of hours ago and are now on a deserted and lonely four-lane road. Few cars pass us in either direction, the radio stations are all heavily laced with static, and we have no cell phone reception. I guess we're in what is referred to as the middle of nowhere to all but those who live in the area. Melinda, truly sincere but downhearted again, says "I can't believe we're still in Texas!"

"Yes, Melinda." I snap. "For the fourth time this morning we are still in Texas! It's a big state!"

At this point, I must admit, I can't believe we're still in Texas, either. If all had gone according to my road-warrior plan, we would be in Colorado by now.

"You don't have to be so bitchy," she snaps back. "I hate being in a car this long. I want to get home. I can't believe I had to do this. Why did I have to drive back with all these dogs?"

She's clearly beyond frustrated and on the verge of tears. I'm right there with her. The grueling journey has worn us both to our core and we are growing tense with one another.

"Whatever!" I had slowed slightly to listen to her, but now I slam down on the accelerator. With the rapid increase in speed, the van swerves ever so slightly. We hear the loud ba-bump, ba-bump, ba-bump warning alerting me that I have left the paved road and am on the shoulder. I pull off the shoulder quickly, straighten the wheel and within seconds we hear a loud "Pow!" The van swerves wildly and all I can see in the rearview mirror are the dogs bouncing in every direction behind us. As I slow the van, it starts vibrating to the familiar wobble-wobble-wobble of a flat tire. Great. So much for divine intervention.

"No freaking way!" I fight the shuddering steering wheel as I slow the wobbling van. We limp down the highway and I pull off at the first exit and guide us onto the grassy shoulder. We sit in stunned silence. The road is truly desolate. No buildings can be seen in either direction, just field after field of tall weeds. It's too remote and unforgiving, even for farmers.

I silently sum up our situation. There are few if any cars on the road, we're out in the middle of nowhere, it's incredibly hot, we have a flat tire, no cell service, and nine dogs beginning to pant. The dogs, of course, think it's time to get out of the car and run and play. They all start jumping on and off the seats, climbing on top of each other and fighting their way to the front seat.

"Carpe freakin' diem!" I want to cry.

Melinda looks at me. "What are we going to do?" I really feel sorry for her. She hadn't bought into this. I always volunteer to drive rescued dogs anywhere they need to go, but Melinda is on this trip purely by default. She got the short straw but she hadn't been the one to pick it.

"I guess I need to call the car rental agency—this totally sucks!" I bang the steering wheel and draw back my hand in pain. It's a serious situation and my anxiety level is already high. I can't have a meltdown right now. It won't help the situation, but it will cause Melinda added stress if she has to deal with the situation and me.

"How are you going to call someone? We have no cell service." We both stare ahead again for a few moments. The dogs' panting steadily increases as the Texas heat fills the van. I open the door, climb up the narrow hood and onto the van roof and hold my cell phone to the sky. Nothing.

"Give me your cell," I call down to Melinda. She tosses her phone up to me and I hold it high. No signal. As I pull the phone back in, I notice a faint bleep of a bar. I wait. After a few minutes I get two bars, then four bars. Then they disappear. I realize I can get some cell reception, although it's weak, but at least we have a chance to communicate with someone.

"Yes!" I yell ecstatically. "Give me the car company's phone number, quick! I have a signal."

"Wait!" There is concern in Melinda's voice. "What are we going to do when they get here and see that we have nine dogs? We'll be busted! What if they say we can't take them all in their rental?"

"I hadn't thought of that!" I jump off the hood of the van and get back in the front seat. The heat has already caused our faces to flush and perspiration rolls down our temples. The dogs are panting harder in the thick, hot air.

"Well, we'll just have to deal with it when they get here." I'm determined. "They can't just abandon us here in the middle of nowhere, can they? Could you see the headlines? Rental car agency abandons good Samaritans and nine rescued Katrina dogs on side of Texas highway in one hundred degree heat."

We both laugh and I dial the rental agency's number. Luck jumps back on our side. It's Saturday and there is only one employee working at the rental agency. She apologetically tells us that she will have to send a tow truck out with a new van for us. The tow truck will then take the van with the flat and return it to Dallas. It's great news. No rental agency representative will be coming out! Then she gives me the bad news. It will take the tow truck at least an hour and a half to get to us. I plead with the agent to make it as fast as she can, and she says she'll do what she can, but makes no promises.

Suddenly it seems a lot hotter. The tame morning sun has risen to quickly become a harsh noonday sun. It sits on top of us, blazing down, roasting us in the vehicle. The air-conditioner provides no relief, as it blows warm air with the engine off. We have no choice but to sit in the scorching Texas heat.

We know we have to get the dogs out of the heat. One by one, we take each dog out and walk them through the dry brown weeds alongside the road. We walk them back to the van, give them water and trudge them through more knee-high weeds and sharp stickers to a nearby rickety wooden fence, where we tie them. After we finish walking them, Melinda lets Cujo out of his crate, again leash-free. He starts doing his happy dance, prancing around the empty road.

Then, without warning, he takes off and runs up the berm that leads to the highway.

"No! Oh, no! Melinda!" I throw the bottled water I'm drinking and take off running. "Get Cujo! Help me get Cujo!"

We race up the berm and onto the highway, chasing the little devil dog. This time I'm grateful the highway is deserted. Melinda catches up with him and scoops him up into her arms. He immediately nips her. Adrenalin runs high from the impromptu sprint and we're both panting, me far more than she is. My lungs haven't yet recovered from the effects of chemotherapy and are nowhere near normal capacity, especially when compared to the athlete that Melinda is. I'm completely winded and dizzy from the sprint and heat. I bend down on one knee on the shoulder with the sun beating down on me. I bend my head down and the perspiration drips off my body, each drip hitting the sand making miniature mud pies below me.

I consider laying down right here on the side of the road, closing my eyes and wishing it all away. I'm almost ready to resign myself to the fact that circumstance has gotten the better of me. These thoughts have barely cleared my mind and I'm pulling myself up, scolding myself and remembering that when things are tough you don't lie down in the sand, wallow in self pity and wish you were somewhere else. Guess what? I'm not. I've been through worse than this and look where I am. My thoughts travel to my beloved Hannah, Hanuman and Bella. I miss them terribly and can't wait to get home to see them, hold them, hug them. It has been a long road, starting with Hannah's misdiagnosis and then my real diagnosis. All the surgeries, chemo sessions and radiation flash through my mind in an instant. Then the devastation of New Orleans. This is nothing.

My panting subsides and I wipe the sweat off my almost-bald head, regretting the throwing of my water bottle. This really is nothing compared to what could face us. *Buck up little camper,* I tell myself. That phrase has always made me smile and now lightens my mood. I stand up and walk back to the van, holding my side, breathless. I sit in the hot sand next to the van and try to catch my breath.

"Leash him now." It's all I can get out between gasps. I'm not happy, thinking of what could have happened.

An hour later, Melinda and I still sit on the side of the road, hot, tired and bored. I'm lost in thought, yearning for my cool, dry Colorado climate. The dogs lined up along the fence now nap in the sun. Every once in awhile, one of us douses them with a bit of water and they don't like it. I wonder if it has anything to do with the recent flood they endured, but it's necessary to keep them cool. We decide to unpack everything so that when the new van arrives, we can quickly load up and be on our way.

It takes only five minutes to clear out the van. We step back and look up at the huge stack of dog crates on the roof.

"What do you want to do?" Melinda asks.

"I'll climb up and throw them down to you. I can do that without raising my arms too high." I once again jump onto the hood of the van. Sweat drips onto the hot metal as I climb up the windshield to the roof, undo the bungee cords and start tossing the plastic crate sections down.

Once done, we stand back and survey our domain. It's quite a scene, like the aftermath of a tornado. Paper bags, suitcases, coolers, dog crates, clothing, food, maps, books and dog supplies are strewn alongside the road next to a van with a flat tire. Cujo sits amid the mess, tied to Melinda's luggage, and eight dogs look at us in utter confusion while tied to the fence at the perimeter.

We have nothing to do but sit and wait. We make seats out of a cooler and suitcase and try to lie back and sun ourselves, passing the time sharing idle conversation. We hear a plane and both look to the sky as a jet passes overhead.

"I bet that's Sam and Cheryl. We could have been with them," Melinda playfully pouts. She's right. It's all so ridiculous. We watch the jet soar away and laugh at the irony of it. I think the heat has made us delirious. Two hours and three rental agency calls later, we continue to watch the horizon.

Staring out at nothing, we suddenly notice movement in the distance. Through waves of heat ricocheting off the highway, we finally see a stubby crane-like apparatus above the cab of a truck and realize it is a tow truck. As it gets closer, we see a van on the back of the truck and I silently pray this isn't yet another false alarm. Several times over the last couple of hours, we have seen an approaching truck and excitedly jumped up, thinking our rescuer had arrived. Each time, the truck passed by leaving us standing, bags in hand, eating the dust and grime that flew in our faces as the truck blew by us. This time, a blinker goes on and the truck slowly exits the highway.

The guy driving the tow truck couldn't have been nicer. He gives us an odd look when he first pulls up. We must be a sight, the dogs and all our belongings strewn along the roadside. As he unloads the van from the back of his truck, we tell him the story of how we came to be stranded on the highway with nine dogs.

We describe working at the shelter in Louisiana, rescuing the dogs, driving from Baton Rouge and end the story with our flat tire. The driver helps us load everything into the new van and starts to load the dog crates on the roof, only to discover the roof rack is different than our original van and the crates won't fit. He could have politely excused himself and left us there, but instead he takes pity on us and quickly reconfigures the crates. Within minutes, he has loaded them on the roof and secured them with the bungee cords. We thank him profusely, give him a nice tip and begin to load the dogs into the new van. We are ecstatic! Almost three hours after getting the flat tire, we're loaded up and once again on the road. The air-conditioned van is quiet and cool, a welcome relief to our and the dogs' overheated bodies. We ride in silence for an hour or two, not even listening to the radio.

Just outside Wichita Falls, my phone rings. It's Seth. I remember that I hadn't returned his call from earlier this morning. I answer and he is as pleasant as can be, albeit a bit more reserved than usual. He's calling to let us know that the dogs Bland and Jan accompanied have arrived at the shelter and are settled in their kennels. He asks how many more dogs we have.

"We have nine," I tell him, cautiously.

"So I heard." He isn't happy and understandably so. "I'm not sure what you expect me to do with all these dogs."

I can't drive and talk, so I hand the phone to Melinda. I listen as she and Seth discuss the dogs, but the phone keeps cutting in and out. Melinda hits the End button and tosses the phone onto the dashboard.

"I think Seth's pissed," she says nonchalantly.

"Why?" The last thing I want right now is to have someone angry with me.

"I don't know, something about us bringing back too many dogs. He said he told you to only bring back eight or nine and we have eighteen." Melinda seems unconcerned and continues to look at the map she holds.

"Yes, we have eighteen dogs. . . ." I start, only to be interrupted as my cell phone rings.

Melinda grabs the ringing phone. "It's Bland. Hey Bland . . . Yeah, I know, he just called us but we went out of range. I know he's pissed—"

I interrupt. "Tell her to call Seth and tell him that we're not bringing eighteen dogs to him." We had only brought nine dogs for him. "Tell him the others are dogs that people have asked us to bring back to them. They're not going to the shelter."

I feel like I'm in big trouble and have to defend my actions.

Melinda relays my message to Bland and hangs up the phone. "She's going to call him, let him know that not all eighteen dogs will be at his shelter and hope he's okay with it." Truth be told, all eighteen dogs are going to the animal shelter. They have to. They'll need to be processed as intakes and its Seth's responsibility to make sure they are.

Melinda goes back to reading the map.

"Yes, Melinda, we're still in Texas." I smile warmly at her as she stares at the big state covering two atlas pages.

Several hours later I'm driving along, lost in thought when Melinda bursts out happily, "Look! New Mexico! We're not in Texas anymore!" She screams as we cross the state line. I look away from the road just in time to catch the familiar "Welcome to New Mexico Land of Enchantment" sign signifying our long-awaited departure from Texas.

"Yeah baby, we're almost home!" I shout, equally as happy. My mind quickly calculates time and distance. "We should be home by nine or ten o'clock tonight! Yippee! I can't wait!"

We drive along the lonely stretch of road in the upper northeast corner of New Mexico that seems to serve no other purpose than to connect Texas to Colorado. It is fairly desolate, dry and sandy. Tumbleweed blows along the roadside and there is only the occasional shrub or sagebrush. In the distance, I see a comforting and familiar outcropping that I remember from my frequent trips from Austin to Aspen. I think it's Capulin Mountain, but it's always been "Volcano Rock" to me. It's nowhere near the size of a Colorado mountain, but I guess if you're surrounded by sand, rock and shrubs, it can be construed as a mountain.

Before too long, I see the familiar shady silhouettes on the horizon and my face melts into a satisfied smile. The Rocky Mountains. I love the mountains and have always felt a deep connection with them, which only deepened when I moved to Aspen. They always signified home to me even when I didn't live in Colorado. I let out a deep sign and then slowly inhale. I can breathe . . . finally, I can breathe. I can almost smell and taste the Colorado air.

We drive through Raton, leaving New Mexico, and cross into Colorado.

"Melinda . . ." I sing, ". . . we're definitely not in Texas anymore! We're as good as home!"

The sun hangs low on the horizon as we exit I-25 and start the beautiful drive through Walsenburg that will eventually take us up to Independence Pass. If you live in the Aspen area, once you reach "the Pass," you consider yourself home.

I decide to stop for gas and a snack so we can make the rest of the drive home without having to stop. Melinda is excited and ready to shop. She has an uncanny ability to shop anywhere. I was once with her on a road trip to Santa Fe and she actually bought an oil painting at a gas station in the middle of nowhere. As I start to pump gas, she flings the car door open wide and absent-mindedly turns to say something to me.

"Melinda!" Dogs start jumping out of the car. "Close the freakin' door! Get the dogs!"

I abandon the gas pump and we both chase four dogs that have escaped. As we run, I yell, "Slow, don't run, we're scaring them!"

After five minutes of herding the loose dogs and bribing them with treats and baby-talk, we gently coax them back to us and put them in the van. I close my eyes and silently count my blessings. With nine dogs, we're lucky that only four escaped and they came back to us and didn't head for the hills or the highway.

Fifteen minutes later, I drive along, lost in the beauty of the area. This swath of Colorado is a hidden gem. Tucked half-way between the interstate and the mountains, we drive through lush, emerald green meadowlands and sparsely-located farmhouses that look like they were designed by Norman Rockwell. As I take in the surrounding beauty, Melinda turns and starts counting. She stops at eight and starts again. Again, she stops at eight.

"Oh, no!" She looks at me, clearly panicked. "I think we're missing a dog!"

"What? Who are we missing?" I slam on the brakes. Dirt and rocks fly up behind us as I quickly pull the van onto the shoulder of the narrow road.

"I don't know, but I really think we only have eight dogs."

We both turn around and quickly count the dogs. Eight! Crap! Unnerved, I'm about to swing the van around and race back to the gas station when I see two little eyes peering out from under the pile of dogs on the back seat. It's Hedy Lamar, silent and forgotten, yet again. She's barely visible, buried under dogs and blankets.

Still not completely confident that we're all together and ready to continue the journey, we both count the dogs again. " . . . seven, eight, nine!" Yes! There are nine—life is good. We sit for a moment on the shoulder of the road to regain our composure. Without saying another word, I put the car in drive and take off down the highway.

The sun sets over the mountains. Nightfall is upon us. Driving these back roads at night is treacherous, since wildlife tends to graze on the side of the road and will frequently dart out in front of speeding cars. I roll the window down and let in some cool mountain air. I smile at how different it smells, a far cry from the hot, pungent, muggy nights in Louisiana. I love the way it smells and feels, clean and woodsy and crisp and alive. I breathe the air in deeply, filling my nostrils and lungs and feel refreshed.

We turn towards Twin Lakes and beyond that, the drive over Independence Pass. In some ways, I'm glad it's dark outside so that I can't see the steep drop-offs that are a constant on this stretch of narrow road. The drive over the Pass, on a good day, can be a nail biter. The road twists and turns up the Continental Divide with sheer drop-offs and few guardrails. I remember my first trip over the Pass—I was so nervous my palms were literally sweating. I wasn't driving and was so scared I was almost in tears. I would scream "slow down!" to my boyfriend at the time, if he dared to go over 20 miles per hour. Some of the more dangerous curves have 10 mph posted speed limits. As he drove, I watched the speedometer. If he hit 12 mph, I would scold him or dig my nails into the armrest and let out a huff of air. It was the first and last time I let someone drive me over the Pass. From that day until only recently, I took the Pass only if I was the one at the wheel.

Tonight is different. I'm exhausted and can't wait to get home. Melinda and I have switched seats and she is now driving. It's funny how the mind prioritizes things. On a normal day, I would have insisted on driving. Tonight is far from normal. I couldn't care less who is driving. Melinda has lived in Aspen far longer than me, and she cruises the road effortlessly. With the cloak of darkness upon us, I can't see the steep drop-offs, so it's a case of out of sight, out of mind. Just get me home! It's true what they say: the last leg of a journey is most definitely the longest.

It's almost 11 p.m. as we summit the Pass. We're greeted with a breathtakingly beautiful sight. On this clear, cold night, stars blanket the sky, their dazzling brilliance only slightly overshadowed by an almost full moon. The shadowy outline of the surrounding mountain peaks provide a slightly eerie backdrop. We are alone here, not a soul anywhere near to us. It is magnificent to be at the very top of the Continental Divide at midnight. The moonlight reflects off a light dusting of newly fallen snow and crisply illuminates everything—the trees, mountains and rivers that have been reduced to thin rails of rushing water under the ice stretching out from the banks. If you have never experienced a walk in the mountains, late at night and under a full moon, it is definitely something to put on your bucket list. The beauty is indescribable, beyond words, and must be experienced to understand.

The dogs sleep soundly, Melinda is quiet and there is no cell phone reception, only the night and the moon, stars and snow. The snow! I realize we're in snow; it won't be long before winter is upon us. I can't wait! After the long, hot ten days we have just endured, I yearn for winter and snowfall.

It's almost midnight when we finally pull into Aspen. The town is dark and still. I'm only minutes from seeing my own beloved dogs and am filled with so much anticipation I can barely contain myself. I have missed them terribly and cannot wait to see and hug them. It will be nice to sleep in my own bed with them in their usual spots, surrounding me.

We roll through the near-empty streets and start discussing who will take which dogs home. Melinda and I divide up the dogs based on who we think will get along with whom. We decide Melinda will take Sweetie, Stella, Jethro, Ellie Mae and Cujo; I'll take the rest. We both have very small, fenced-in yards, but we'll only have the dogs until early morning, when we take them to the shelter. From there . . . from there, where? Most of them will likely be placed into foster homes and finally regain some sense of normalcy. I am so, so, so very happy to be home.

A few hours before I arrived, my brother left for his own place, assured I would be home during the night. The house is dark except for a dim light glowing through the kitchen window. I try to very quietly unlock my door, hoping I can sneak inside without waking my dogs.

It doesn't work. With the very first click of the lock, there is ferocious barking from within and what sounds like a herd of wildlife trampling toward me.

"Hush, shhhh . . . babies, it's only me."

The barking immediately turns into whines and squeals of delight as Hanuman, Hannah and Bella realize I have returned home. I can barely make it inside the door before I am squashed against the wall, buried in dog licks, bouncing fur and affectionate nuzzling. All three dogs whimper and whine, Hannah's butt wiggles ferociously, Bella's tail wags a mile a minute, and even my sweet, usually somber Hanuman starts bucking excitedly.

I slide down the wall and embrace them all. "Hi, hi, hi . . . oh, sweeties, I've missed you so much! Yes, I'm home! Missed you, missed you, missed you!" I hold and kiss each one on their nose.

The love fest lasts less than a minute before the sniffing starts. I'm sure I must be a smorgasbord of doggie smells, some delightful, some not. Their noses wildly explore every inch of my body, breathing in and huffing out.

I sit with them for about ten minutes and relish finally being back home. Then I close them in my bedroom so I can bring in the Katrina dogs. Once they're settled, I quietly go back into my bedroom. Despite the late hour, I indulge in a hot shower before slipping into bed and blissfully snuggling my face into the fur of my dogs, my own dogs. I couldn't be happier.

Chapter 12

MY FIRST DAY BACK STARTS far too early as the phone rings before 8 a.m. It is Seth, letting me know that the dogs are something of celebrities and there's a line of people at the shelter waiting to see them. Most hope for a chance to foster one. I assure him I will get up and down there as fast as I can.

Instead of getting up, though, I lie in bed for a moment and reflect on my conversation with him the day before. I'm concerned about Melinda and I bringing the nine dogs to him this morning. I know we've pushed him beyond his limits, both literally and figuratively. However, this is a time when most of us are being pushed beyond our limits as we step up and try to help. I know Seth better than most. I know his heart and his passions, and I know that if he is or was a bit angry, he won't be angry for long. He has something of a routine. He will initially freak out at trying situations in which we place him, but he has a tendency to quickly rise above the fray and deal with whatever is in front of him. He gets it.

My phone rings again. I recognize the number on the caller ID. "What's up?" I ask sleepily.

"One of the dogs ran away." Melinda sounds panicked.

I jerk up in bed. "What?" My sudden action startles my dogs out of their sleep. They get up and start milling about anxiously.

"He jumped my fence when I put him outside this morning. He ran away."

"What?" I repeat, astounded. "Who? Which one?"

My mind is reeling, trying to remember which dogs she kept, and which of those is capable of jumping her fence. Our conversation is interrupted by the first of what will become a constant string of beeps, signifying incoming calls. I ignore them to deal with this current crisis.

"The brown one . . . the big, brown one . . . Jethro . . ." Her voice trails off as if she's distracted, maybe looking out her windows.

"Oh, no." I groan. "Melinda, of all dogs. What if he bites someone?"

I throw off my bed covers and wade through all the dogs while still talking to her. My mind is jumbled in a tired, mental fog and I can't think clearly. I try to figure out what is more important in this immediate moment, letting the seven dogs out to pee, continuing my conversation with Melinda, answering the incoming calls, or getting dressed and flying out the door in search of Jethro. In my current state of mindlessness, they all seem equally important and I can't decide. I can't even comprehend my name right now.

"I know, I'm sorry . . ." Her voice trails off again.

Chatting is definitely the last thing to do. "When was the last time you saw him?"

"I let him out a few minutes ago and when I went to get him he was gone."

"Alright, have you called Seth to let him know?"

"No." I can tell by her tone that she does not want to make that call.

"Animal control?" I ask, hopeful she has at least called them.

"No . . . I didn't know what to do, so I called you first."

She's really upset. Badgering her won't help the situation, but only exacerbate it. I lighten up. "Let me call Seth and I'll get dressed and be right over."

"Okay, thanks." She sounds disheartened.

I switch to the incoming call. It is Seth. "Hey, sorry to call again how are you?" His voice is harried and words run together so I know he must be busy. ". . . I need to let people know when the dogs will arrive. Do you know what time you'll be bringing them in?"

"Melinda lost one of the dogs . . ." I respond, ignoring his question, "It jumped her fence."

"You're kidding!" he responds. "No way!"

"Yep! Any calls?" I ask, hopeful.

"No." His voice trails off and I can tell he is truly concerned. "Let me call dispatch for you and see if they've had any calls. I'll call you right back."

I wade through the dogs, grabbing articles of clothing along the way. My dogs are being very clingy and territorial with me, having not seen me in over ten days. I have to remember to pay attention to them alone, at least for a few minutes. I want to keep things calm because if I don't and one of the other dogs growls, barks or snarls, it could lead to a fur-flying fight between my brood and the Katrina dogs.

I let the four Katrina dogs into the backyard and head to the bathroom with my clothes, shoes and toothbrush. Within minutes, I'm dressed and head outside to let in the Katrina dogs and send my three outside. Just as I open the door, I notice my landlord in my backyard. He is a short, thin, balding man, clad in a safari hat, khaki shorts, tank top, white knee socks and hiking boots. He holds a shovel in one hand and a paper shopping bag in the other. A scowl crosses his face. He catches my eye as I stand in the doorway, peaking through a crack in the sliding glass door.

"Anne . . ." he starts, obviously irritated. "What's going on? Whose dogs are these? Look at this, there's poop all over the yard. I want to get in here and mow."

He stares past me, aware of the commotion behind me as my dogs react to his tone by barking ferociously.

"You know, a little notice would have been nice, as I've asked you before." I'm really not in the mood for confrontation.

He ignores my snippiness. With his hand and brown bag perched high on his tilted hip, he surveys the yard. "Look at this, where did all this dog poop come from?" He turns, giving me a distasteful look.

"Can you excuse me and I'll clean it so you can mow? I just got back from New Orleans late last night and these are rescued dogs. We didn't get in until after midnight, so they had to stay here with me, but I'm taking them to the animal shelter in a few minutes." I feel slightly rebellious.

He reacts as I assume he will—by turning around and walking off in a huff. I don't care. I shut the sliding glass door and head to the front door, so I can start loading the Katrina dogs into the van. I want to get them to the shelter quickly so I can join in the search for Jethro.

As I make my way toward the door, the phone rings. Seth. "Dispatch just called. They have reports of a large reddish-brown dog running loose by the post office—"

"—I'm on my way over there. I'll call you back." I hang up the phone and race out the door. I'm in a full sprint and nearly run my landlord down as he rounds the corner of the house. "Too bad you don't treat your own dogs as well as you treat those other dogs, leaving them here . . ."

He realizes the impact of his words as they're leaving his mouth, but it is too late to retract them.

I straddle the car door, about to get in. His words hit a nerve and infuriate me. I already feel guilty that I have left my own dogs for ten days and am now running off again. In this moment, it doesn't matter that my brother, Mike, whom they adore, had been doggie-sitting them. I feel terrible that I haven't spent much time with them—even though I shouldn't feel that way. My dogs are well cared for, get plenty of exercise and attention and are loved immensely. Still, my landlord's words sting deeply and I can't contain myself.

I slam the car door without getting in. "What are you talking about?" I ask, fire in my eyes. I'm incensed. "How could you say something like that! You have no idea what you're talking about. I was just down in New Orleans for ten days taking care of abandoned Katrina pets while you sat here and worried about whether your grass was half an inch higher than it should be. How dare you criticize me? My dogs are well taken care of. Please!"

I get in the car, slam the door and squeal out of the driveway. He stands there, stunned and speechless, watching me drive off.

I'm barely out of the driveway and I'm sobbing. Although I know I'm the farthest thing from it, I wonder if I'm a terrible pet owner. Are my own dogs suffering as I try to save these others? A clear and rational answer would be a resounding "No!" but in my current fragile, emotional state, I can't think straight. I am overly-sensitive, a mixed-up bundled of fatigue, sadness over the separation from my own dogs, panic at having to find the lost dog and stress at knowing people are waiting at the shelter to see the dogs I have left at my house. I thought being home would bring some semblance of relaxation, the satisfaction of a job well done.

This is all too much. I almost wish I were back in New Orleans, away from all my responsibilities here. Almost, but not quite. As I reach the corner and look in my rearview mirror, my landlord walks slowly toward his house, shovel and bag in hand, looking downtrodden. He should feel bad. He had never seen this side of me, but I'm only slightly ashamed at showing it.

I race the few blocks to the post office, but there is no one around when I arrive. I head up the road toward Main Street. Halfway up the block I see a City of Aspen police car and Melinda's SUV. Both vehicles are pulled off the road by a large parking area, atop a tall brick wall. In the far corner of the lot, I see Melinda and Dave, one of Aspen's finest and friendliest police officers, trying to catch Jethro. They have him backed into a corner and he snarls at them while eyeing the wall behind him.

I stop the car, jump out and race toward them. As soon as I

get close, I can feel Jethro's energy and know he's contemplating jumping the wall. Unfortunately and unbeknownst to him, the other side of the wall drops off. If he jumps, he could injure himself. I'm afraid when he sees me coming toward him, he'll feel even more threatened and jump.

Again, he surprises me. When he sees me, he immediately becomes a seasoned punt returner, running with great agility between Melinda and Dave, artfully avoiding both of them. He runs toward me, his tail high and wagging. He is so exuberant I'm afraid he'll knock me down. Instead, when he reaches me, he immediately sits at my feet and looks up, sweetly. He is panting heavily. When I lean to pet him, I feel his heart racing. It's clear he's been running a lot this morning, lost and probably scared. I give him a hug and whisper, "What a good boy you are."

Dave and Melinda approach, clearly relieved. "Boy, he likes you." Dave is grinning. It's another nice thing about living in a small town. For all the hype and hoopla about Aspen's stature as a star's playground, underneath, it is a small town with small-town values and people who care. Most of us know one another. All of us feel blessed to have friendly, caring people like Dave on our police force.

"Can you believe it?" I ask, looking up at Dave's smile. "This little guy has been through hell. They found him running around the Superdome ten days after Katrina. Guess his owner was evacuated, but who knows?"

I look down at him, wishing he could talk and tell me everything he'd been through. His big brown eyes beam up at me. "Oh, no. Don't look at me like that." I hug him closer. "I already have three dogs and definitely can't have a fourth! You can't come home with me, buddy, sorry Jethro."

The more I will learn about this dog, the more I will come to realize that the name Jethro does not fit him. It never felt right. It doesn't do him justice, not at all. He's much more dignified than that.

Chapter 13

THE REST OF THE DAY BLURS with activity. We get the dogs settled into the shelter, talk with people about them, send some out to foster homes, talk to a reporter who is running a story in the local newspaper, and try to keep things as together as we can, given the pace. Bland phones me midday and tells me that our two Labs were given to us erroneously and must be immediately returned to Baton Rouge. It seems the dogs belong to someone there, had gotten out of their yard and were mistakenly taken to LSU, where they were put in with the Katrina dogs. Karla at LSU has already made arrangements for the dogs to be flown home, but they need to be taken to Denver tomorrow.

"Seriously?" I can't believe what I'm hearing. I have only just returned from the long, grueling road trip and now someone has to drive the two Labs to Denver. Bland says something, but I can't hear her clearly. My cell phone beeps with incoming calls, and there are people and dogs and too much noise around me.

In the midst of it all, I mentally step back and absorb the commotion around me. A quiet trip to Denver might not be such a bad idea. It would be a chance for a little down time, some quiet isolation.

"I'll go with you." I interrupt whatever Bland is saying.

"Really? You would do that? You just got home." Bland is surprised that I've offered to go.

"I know but I think it might be nice to get out of here for a day. We can make the best of it. After we drop the dogs at the plane, we can have a nice lunch and a quiet, leisurely drive home. The trees on the Pass will be gorgeous and we won't have nine dogs with us." I laugh.

"That's true. I'll do all the driving if you'll go. The dogs have to be at the airport by one." I feel bad leaving my dogs again, but it won't be for long this time. I'll be there and back in seven or eight hours. I was bummed that we drove over the Pass at night because we missed the trees and the spectacular Fall colors. I'm happy that I'll get another chance to see them.

We leave early the next morning and start the drive energetic and chatty. This is the first time Bland and I have been alone long enough to reflect on everything we have been through. As we wind our way up the Pass, the aspen trees live up to our expectations. They are stunning. We become so lost in conversation that when we reach the other side of the Pass, we laugh as we realize we forgot to truly appreciate them after that first glimpse. We vow to admire them more fully on the drive home.

When we reach Leadville and are back in cell range, Bland and I both listen to our messages. We both have panicked calls from the shelter, letting us know that they can't find one of the dogs. They're at a loss—the dog was in a kennel and then, suddenly, was gone. Everyone is stumped. Security is tight at the shelter and it's next to impossible for a dog to escape from one of the kennels, inside or out.

Bland and I look at one another. "Are you getting the same message I am?" I ask.

"Yes, jeez, what could have happened?" We continue to listen to the messages. One of the last messages is Seth, very relieved, letting us know they have found the missing dog. As it turns out, Melinda had come to the shelter and, finding the staff busy helping people, let herself into the back kennel area, took the dog, and gave it to a friend of hers to foster.

We make our way through Denver. As we approach the airport, which is about 30 minutes west of town, I sense sadness in Bland. She has been fostering the old Black Lab and just decided she would formally adopt her. It is hard for her to say good-bye, but it is comforting to know these dogs are going to their rightful home. We make sure their kennels have blankets, water and toys, give them both big, strong hugs, and send them on their way. We're both teary-eyed as we walk out of the hangar and into the warm September sunshine but feel a sense of satisfaction that these two are going home. We stop at a café for lunch, sit outside to enjoy the warm sun, and talk about how hard it is to decompress after New Orleans. It takes a conscious effort, but we both finally begin to relax.

We start our journey home. As we reach the foothills on the outskirts of Denver, I roll the windows down to enjoy the beautiful day. I'm savoring the calmness of the moment when Bland's phone rings. It is Seth letting us know that another Katrina dog, Blackie, is lost. Throughout the next few hours, calls are exchanged. More often than not, we lose signal on the mountainous roads. "So much for relaxation," I huff.

Before long, there is no cell coverage, so we have no choice but to try and relax. It isn't easy, knowing Blackie is missing. I catch my reflection in the window. Only then am I aware that I've been biting my lip, consumed with thoughts of him.

We finally start our descent down the Pass, anxious to return to cell range so we can check on the dogs. When we finally call we find, to our dismay, that Blackie is still lost. We drive as fast as we can.

Once we arrive at the shelter, we get the story: Melinda had left Blackie and her dogs in her car with the window down. Despite swearing it was only cracked a couple inches, the dog was able to make his escape. Now, several small groups of volunteers search for him in the late afternoon. Despite being tired from the trip,

Bland and I agree to meet in a couple hours to continue the search if he is still missing.

That's what happens. Bland and I find ourselves crouched in bushes, calling for the dog. After searching in the darkness for an hour, we resign ourselves to the fact that there is nothing more we can do but give in and go home. We're upset at the thought of Blackie spending the night outside, alone, in unfamiliar territory. Fortunately, early the following morning Melinda manages to locate him and brings him to the shelter. He'll be placed a foster home that day.

Things remain busy for the next week. Not everyone in town is thrilled that we have brought these "potentially diseased" dogs into what they consider our pristine valley. One longtime local writes a letter to the editor trashing us for bringing "Pit Bulls" into town, referring to Jan's dog, Daisy. The letter is horrible and Jan is hurt deeply by it. She adores Daisy, who is a sweet and submissive Pit Bull/Lab mix. The perception that we are bringing in diseased or aggressive dogs is ignorant and ill-informed. We would not bring unadoptable dogs into our shelter, especially when there were so many wonderful homeless dogs in New Orleans needing rescue. A part of me wonders how people can have so little compassion, but I quickly remind myself it is only a few people who feel this way. The vast majority of locals, and certainly the shelter supporters, are grateful for our work.

We continue with what will become a very long process of trying to find the dogs' owners. Of the eighteen dogs we brought back, the two Labs have been returned to Baton Rouge and the four puppies had no prior homes, so we're looking for twelve owners.

Bland carries the brunt of the work. She spends hours posting all the dogs on Petfinders and looking through the thousands of listings that have been posted to see if she can match any up. A few of the dogs have rabies tags, so we try to track them through vet offices. Unfortunately, this is impossible, since we can't get through to most southern Louisiana numbers. If, by chance, we are lucky enough to dial a number and it actually rings, there is no answer. Like most of the city, the vet offices have long been deserted. We continue to hold onto hope, determined to do everything in our power to find the owners.

The dogs enter foster homes. Despite many pleas, we refuse to let anyone adopt any of the dogs, except the puppies. We know that it is far too soon to give up. These pets need and deserve to be reunited with their families. We'll only adopt them out to new families as a last resort.

We remove the collars and tags from the dogs and Bland meticulously logs them onto individual charts, which contain any and all information, old and new, on each dog. Bland logs information as significant as microchip numbers, medical history and current treatments, and as minimal as a call that lead nowhere.

As I sit on the floor at the shelter, looking at the dog charts, a young guy walks in. He appears to be in his early twenties and tells Seth he would like to adopt a dog. I'm not really paying much attention until I notice him spending a lot of time in front of Jethro's kennel. Jethro has been one of the harder dogs to place, given his fearful nature. He doesn't immediately warm up to people, but once someone spends a bit of time with him, he will tolerate and then grow to love them. When I'm around, he doesn't take his eyes off me, so I try to make myself scarce when someone shows interest in him.

The young man tells Seth he'd like information on Jethro. Seth calls me over. The kid seems nice enough, but as we chat he tells me things—he lives close to a highway, has no fence, and lots of company runs in and out of his house. I explain that Jethro will run away if given the slightest chance, and he promises he will keep Jethro on a leash at all times and not let him out of his sight when home. I'm sure my uneasiness stirs from being too attached to the dog. I know I cannot adopt him, so I agree to let the kid foster Jethro.

As soon as they're out the door, I tell Seth that I regret the decision I made. I call the young guy and reiterate that he is only fostering Jethro. I remind him that Jethro must be taken to the vet in two days for his neutering appointment, and I'm not sure if he can have Jethro back after that appointment or not.

Over the course of the next two days, I discover a few things that add to my uneasiness over the potential adoption. I know he will love Jethro, but I'm not convinced he has the skills necessary to handle such a stubborn dog. It is difficult, but I make the decision that Jethro must go back to the shelter.

Because of this decision, I find myself standing at the vet office waiting to get Jethro, as he's been neutered and had his dew claws removed. He is quite the sight as he staggers out. Still drowsy from the anesthesia, his two back legs are bandaged from just above his paws to his knee, and his eyes and forehead droop. His expression immediately changes when he sees me and gingerly makes his way toward me. His big, brown eyes zero in on mine and radiate love. It is in this moment that I realize the depth of my bond with the dog.

I take Jethro home but bring him back to the shelter every day, trying to find the perfect home for him. Time after time, as each prospective fosterer takes him on a walk, he tries to turn back, tugging hard at his leash. When he returns from each walk, he is overjoyed to see me.

After four days of this routine, a quiet, middle-aged couple comes in to see him. There's something I like about them, and I feel they might be the perfect family for Jethro. They have a nice home in the mountains with a large, fenced yard and, more importantly, I can tell they are especially fond of dogs. As they take Jethro for a walk, I hide behind my car to watch. He sees me and starts his usual tugging. The couple walks a very short distance and, while still in view, they turn around and head back to me.

"Do you see how attached this dog is to you? We can't take him;

it's obvious he wants to be with you." The woman hands the leash back to me.

I take his leash. "Oh, no . . . I can't have a fourth dog." I stammer. It's probably the tenth time I've said the words, but it's the first time I don't really believe them myself.

Back inside the shelter, I sit on the floor and return to working on the dogs' belongings. I come across the stunning Irish Setter's possessions and look through her bag, then again at the tags on her collar. For the first time, I realize that one of her tags is from a military vet. I stare at it and it suddenly occurs to me that this is probably one tag that can be traced. Having grown up as an Air Force brat, I know the military is very strict about paperwork and protocol. There must be some sort of paper trail on the dog.

Bland and I look at the information on the tag. She writes it down and is off and running. Within minutes, she is on the phone, calling military bases and tracking records.

After a couple hours, she calls me, ecstatic. She has found Stella's owner. We also learn that Stella's real name is Lucy. She relays the conversation she had with the owner, a man, and how he became tearful, overcome with emotion, when he discovered his beautiful girl had survived the horrors of Hurricane Katrina. He was thrilled and grateful that she was safe and being cared for and loved. Bland promised to make whatever arrangements necessary to return her to him as quickly as possible.

Bland puts the word out on her network that we need to transport a dog back to Louisiana. She finds a woman shuttling Katrina pets. She plans to leave the Vail area the next day. She is more than happy to take Lucy home. We are overjoyed to reunite a beloved dog with her distressed owner. It motivates us to keep going.

After more detective work and searching, Bland finds the owners of three other dogs. Unfortunately, two tell us they have evacuated and don't have a home. They are overwhelmed with their circumstances and, sadly, tell her they have to relinquish the dogs.

They hope their pets can be adopted into loving homes in Colorado; we assure them they will be. We promise to arrange open adoptions whenever we can so they can continue to communicate with their pets' new owners.

Bland continues to spend hours scouring the dog ads on Petfinders and other sites that list Katrina dogs. When she is not on her computer, she follows potential leads on the telephone. She keeps logs of conversations and potential dog matches, and retains hundreds of emails she receives, reading each one for any clue that might reunite a dog with an owner. There are many false alarms, people who are certain we have their pets, but when we connect with them and exchange details, it quickly becomes apparent we're not holding their dogs.

Bland and I try to find an hour a day to walk our dogs together. Within a week, Jethro starts accompanying us on these daily walks.

"He's so not a Jethro," I tell Bland as we walk along the rocky path through a grove of aspen trees. She agrees and confesses that she never liked the name Jethro.

As we walk along in silence, I watch Jethro ahead of me. He is majestic and proud, a gorgeous specimen. His reddish brown hair shines when the sun hits it, highlighting the black hairs peppering his spine. He races up and down the trail in front of us, always stopping to look back and make sure I am there. He is finally regaining his confidence. I watch him, thinking of the warrior he is to make it through everything. Through it all, he managed to maintain an amazingly sweet and personable disposition, nothing like the snarly dog I first met at Lamar Dixon. To see him now, joyously romping up the mountain trail, I know he has found the perfect home. With me.

"Stryder," I say out loud.

"What?" Bland bends toward me to better hear what I have just said. "Did you say Striker?"

"No . . ." My voice drifts. I'm only half listening to her as I watch him run in the distance. "Stryder. You know, like the warrior."

Epilogue

AS I REFLECT BACK ON my journey, I understand things a bit better. Finding out that you have cancer can be a very scary and alone time. Although surrounded by family, friends, doctors and counselors, nobody is where you are but you. Despite all the genuine words of love, concern and encouragement, it is what you're feeling inside that consumes you. Doubt or hope, fear or confidence. It can be hard to find reassurances, as it was for me. More often than not, the people you talk with or cases you read are not exactly like yours. There are similarities, but rarely is your experience, desire and journey identical. When you search for comfort in the form of answers, you sometimes find what you're looking for, but can easily stumble upon something you hoped you wouldn't see.

What was important to me was that I remained determined to fight the battle. I always believed I would survive. I never considered the other option. I didn't simply go through the motions, but truly believed it. It kept the fire burning, and it was that fire, that will to fight, that kept me alive. I believed and I had faith, hope, trust and, most importantly, friendships and love. I followed my heart and gut to discover what was important—for me to maintain a sense of purpose.

Throughout it all, I continued my volunteer work as a board member of Friends of the Aspen Animal Shelter and embraced my passions. I believed then, as I do now, that the alternative is to risk becoming self-indulgent, immersed in self-pity, or depressed, withdrawn, lost and seemingly adrift.

Friends were crucial to my survival, as was the comfort I found with my dogs and while walking in the mountains. To this day, I distinctly remember what incredible depth and beauty I found in those short walks. The trees took on a gorgeous life, warm and breathing. The mountains on which they grew seemed to pulsate with life. It forever reminds me of what a beautiful place this world can be when we remember to look at it.

One day, not long after being diagnosed, I was feeling particularly low. Knowing my love of mountains, and in an effort to cheer me up, my good friend Adam said to me, "So . . . what if you did discover your cancer was incurable and you were going to die? What would you do? You would embrace life and move to the mountains. Well, guess what? You're here."

What he said wasn't lost on me. No one really knows what tomorrow brings. Live in the moment and appreciate that moment. It has been said many times and many different ways, but I never felt it more than when facing the uncertainties of cancer. Find the beauty within you or where you are—and embrace it.

I continued to follow coverage of the destruction and ensuing difficulties of the New Orleans rebuilding effort. I realized that I, too, was having difficulty rebuilding. I dealt with depression brought on primarily, I believe, by body consciousness issues and my inability to come to terms with what I perceived to be major physical flaws. I was devastated when I lost Hannah and Hanuman to cancer, within a year of one another, and then lost my mother. I couldn't think about romantic relationships; my conversations with Edward became fewer and farther between. We're still good friends and when we speak, there is a genuine kindness and it's obvious that we truly care about one another. Not traveling very far down the romantic road seemed to give us the space to grow closer. Though we sometimes disagree vehemently on animal welfare issues, underneath it all there remains respect, care and admiration. He is always there for me, as I am for him, and that is a gift for which I am grateful.

Bland, Jan, Melinda and I remain close friends who continue to live in the Aspen area. They, too, have faced devastating challenges. Bland lost her cherished and beloved husband, Michael Cooper, as well as one of her much-loved dogs, Cleo. Jan suffered her own breast cancer scare as well as a severe and debilitating shoulder injury when she was pulled to the ground by one of her dogs as it chased a rabbit. Melinda, too, has suffered through the loss of two of her much-loved dogs.

Despite the terrible ordeals, there have been remarkable rebirths. There is a new and vibrant New Orleans, and a new and changed spirit within me that I owe to my experiences there. I discovered so much about myself. I have Stryder, as well as two new rescued dogs. When I look into his eyes and think back to those Hurricane Katrina days, knowing he almost surely would have been killed, my heart is full of love for him. What is more meaningful is the way his gratitude reflects back, carrying more love than I could ever have imagined. That look, that love, saves me, just as I saved him. I know we can't rescue them all, but we can continue to save all of those that we can.

My life was changed by the cancer and enriched by the Katrina experience. The ten days I spent in Louisiana were the best of times, the worst of times and one of the hardest challenges I've ever experienced, all rolled up into one amazing adventure. It was also, by far, the most meaningful thing I have ever done in my life.

When I started out on my journey, I made a conscious decision to remove myself from being a cancer patient and to continue with my life as normally as possible. Katrina produced a burning need inside me that coincided with a deep passion to help animals in need. During those days, all that mattered was what could be done to alleviate the animals' suffering. Out of all the physical and emotional pain and back-breaking work, thousands of pets were saved and some great friendships formed. Everything came together in that devastating event.

That devastation saved me and awakened and saved so many of us.

About the Author

Anne with her rescued dogs Max, Stryder, Haddie and Bella

ANNE GURCHICK has been involved in animal welfare and rescue work for over ten years, having started in Austin, Texas. In 2004, shortly after selling her business, Anne decided to follow her dream and move to the mountains with the hope of working with animals. She relocated to Aspen, Colorado, and quickly became involved with Friends of the Aspen Animal Shelter (FAAS). Anne has served on the board of FAAS for over seven years and was appointed Director of the non-profit in 2009. Less than six months after arriving in Aspen, Anne was diagnosed with stage II breast cancer and successfully battled the disease.

FAAS kicked off an aggressive spay/neuter/rescue campaign in October 2007. Since that time, the campaign has resulted in the neutering of more than 7,000 dogs and cats in Colorado and beyond. In partnership with Seth Sachson, Director of the Aspen Animal Shelter, the non-profit has also rescued well over 1,000 dogs and cats off death row in shelters where they otherwise would be killed due to overcrowding.

Anne currently lives in Aspen, Colorado, with her four rescued dogs, Bella, Stryder (a Katrina rescue dog), Max and Haddie.

Anne Gurchick, Director of the non-profit Friends of the Aspen Animal Shelter (www.dogsaspen.com), encourages you to make a difference by adopting a shelter pet. A portion of the profits from the book will be donated to animal rescue.

Transformation Media Books

Transformation Media Books is dedicated to publishing innovative works that nourish the body, mind and spirit, written by authors whose ideas and messages make a difference in the world.

Please visit our website:

www.TransformationMediaBooks.com
For more information, the latest titles or to purchase direct

Sooner or Later
   Restoring Sanity to Your End-of-Life Care

Damiano deSano Iocovozzi MSN FNP CNS

ISBN: 978-0-9842258-6-6
Retail List: $12.95 USD

Sooner or Later offers patient, family and caregivers a safe place to help process turbulent emotions during the diagnosis phase of a serious or terminal illness and remain sane, rational and in control.

Sooner or Later provides the information and tools to empower patients and their families to seek the appropriate level of care, take control and make good decisions to maintain the best quality of life.

"*Sooner or Later* is a rare treasure. This book shines with compassion, wisdom, humor, and truth. I believe it should be must reading for everyone. Really!"

—Christiane Northrup, M.D. ob/gyn physician
and author of the *New York Times* bestsellers:
Women's Bodies, Women's Wisdom and *The Wisdom of Menopause*

Don't Die without Me! is the eBook version of *Sooner or Later*

New eBook available at Amazon, BarnesandNoble.com, and other fine retailers including http://www.smashwords.com/books/view/105018

Don't Die Without Me! provides the pertinent questions to ask medical specialists written in a way the reader and provider understand.

Don't Go to the Doctor without Me!
Damiano deSano Iocovozzi MSN FNP CNS

New eBook available at Amazon, BarnesandNoble.com, and other fine retailers including http://www.smashwords.com/books/view/95147

Don't Go to the Doctor without Me! is your personal road map through the health care maze from wellness exams to chronic care management, teaching you how to be your own health care advocate. Uninsured or under insured, this book includes important tips on how to get low cost or free services while still receiving the best possible care. All the questions patients should ask.

Healing from Heaven
A Healer's Guide to the Universe

Daniel Ryan, D. C.

ISBN: 978-0-9846359-4-8
Retail List: $16.95 USD

Cultivate your connection with Spirit via the extraordinary gifts and vast experience of spiritual medium, Dr. Daniel Ryan, known as "Doctor to the Stars."

- Learn to trust your intuition
- Act upon the potential already within you
- See beyond your own belief system
- Open up to inter-dimensional communication and healing
- Tap into your soul's qualities that are yearning to be expressed

Read personal stories of connecting with departed loved ones who helped facilitate healing. *Healing from Heaven* will help you overcome spiritual and energetic blockages to activate and realize authentic freedom, peace of mind, and the love and joy inherent in our nature.

Shift Happens!
Reinvent Yourself Using Innovative Solutions

James D. Feldman

ISBN: 978-0-9846359-4-8
Retail List: $15.95 USD
New eBook available at Amazon, BarnesandNoble.com, and other fine retailers including http://www.smashwords.com/books/view/60296

When Shift Happens you can manage it or let it manage you. Succeeding after shifts in his own life, Feldman illustrates how to stop limiting yourself, retake control and immediately start using change to your advantage. Want to break free of the past, boost your energy, and impact the future? Learn how to apply 3D Thinking to discover innovative solutions in times of high velocity change.

Sereni-Tea
  Sipping Self Success

Dharlene Marie Fahl

ISBN: 978-0-9844600-3-8
Retail List Prices: $15.95 USD,
$17.00 CAD, £ 12.95 GBP

Certified tea specialist, Dharlene Marie Fahl, guides you on an inner journey of self-discovery through the simple practice of sipping tea. Quiet your mind, open your heart and nurture your being as you drink in the peace of self success. Anywhere, anytime, your cup of Sereni-Tea awaits you.

> "*Sereni-Tea* is not a typical book about tea. Yes, it contains all the necessary information to help both novices and experts alike to better appreciate this near-miraculous beverage, but then it uses tea as a means for discovering who we are and what we could become . . ."
> —Joe Simrany, President, Tea Association of the USA

Dying for a Change

William L. Murtha

ISBN: 978-0-9823850-8-1
Retail List: $19.95 USD

Dying for a Change is the gripping, true account of William L. Murtha's fight to survive hypothermia in the freezing waters off the coast of Britain. At a crucial time when his life was rapidly spiraling out of control, William was swept out to sea by a twenty-foot freak wave. Drowning, losing consciousness and convinced that this was the end, he relived many pivotal moments from his past and experienced a life-changing conversation with a Higher Presence.

William's compelling message inspires readers to come face-to-face with their own deepest fears and challenges perceptions about God, life, death and miracles.

> "An amazing story! . . . takes away any doubt that there is an energy force out there ready to help us find our way . . . we need only listen."
> —Susan Jeffers, Ph.D, Author, *Feel the Fear and Do It Anyway*®

The Key of Life
A Metaphysical Investigation

Randolph J. Rogers

ISBN: 978-0-9823850-9-8
Retail List: $18.95 USD

Newsman Randy Rogers takes you along on his riveting journey investigating past lives, present events and reincarnation. Randy proves that "ordinary" people can experience the extraordinary when they open themselves to the possibilities.

The Key of Life is a true story about who we are, why we are here and how we are all connected.

". . . a consciousness-raising self-help detective story . . ."

—Peter Michalos, Author of *Psyche, a Novel of the Young Freud*

". . . a very personal and life changing experience . . . We emerge from it . . . enlightened, inspired."

—Maria Shriver, First Lady of California, Author

EAT IT UP!
The Complete Mind/Body/Spirit Guide
to a Full Life After Weight Loss Surgery

Connie Stapleton, Ph. D.

ISBN: 978-0-9823850-7-4
Retail List: $15.95 USD

Eat It Up! is the first book incorporating a whole person, mind/body/ spirit approach to prevent weight regain in the months and years following weight loss surgery. Written with humor, compassion and a "firm and fair" approach, *Eat It Up!* is a must-have for the millions who are obese or overweight.

"*Eat It Up!* is a must-have book for surgical weight loss patients. Dr. Stapleton goes beyond the "how to" of maintaining weight loss following surgery to providing skills, wisdom and the support necessary to create a fully healthy and balanced life."

—John C. Friel, Ph.D., Licensed Psychologist,
New York Times best-selling author

Tragedy in Sedona
    My Life in James Arthur Ray's Inner Circle

Connie Joy

ISBN: 978-0-9845751-6-9
Retail List: $18.95 USD

Follow Connie Joy inside the seminars and once-in-a-lifetime trips to Egypt and Peru for an up close look at the transformative work of a charismatic teacher—and the underlying danger of mixing up the message with the messenger!

Connie and her husband attended 27 events over three years presented by James Arthur Ray, "Rock Star of Personal Transformation." In 2007, Connie participated in Ray's sweat lodge, a Native American ceremonial sauna meant to be a place of spiritual renewal and mental and physical healing. In reality it was just a test of human endurance for Connie and the other participants. Her prediction that someone could be seriously hurt came true in October 2009 when three people died and 18 participants were injured during a sweat lodge run by James Arthur Ray and his staff.

After injuries at his previous events, why didn't Ray get the message he was literally playing with fire?

After a four month trial, Ray was convicted of three counts of negligent homicide and began serving two years in prison in November, 2011 on each count concurrently. He also is facing a wrongful death suit for the suicide of Colleen Conaway at one of his seminars ten weeks prior to the sweat lodge deaths.

> "James Ray's debut in the film, *The Secret,* thrust him into the spotlight . . . appearances on *Oprah* and *Larry King Live* . . . *Tragedy in Sedona* is a behind the scenes look at the rise and fall of the James Ray Empire, through the eyes of an ultimately disenchanted follower.
>
> Connie Joy takes you on her personal and authentic journey—from being a devoted member of James' inner circle and Dream Team to . . . trying to warn others."
>
> —From the Foreword by forensic psychiatrist Dr. Carole Lieberman

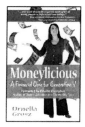

Moneylicious
A Financial Clue for Generation Y

Ornella Grosz

ISBN: 978-0-9845751-1-4
Retail List: $12.95 USD

Spend and invest your hard-earned dollars in an effective way! *Moneylicious* is an easy-to-understand guide for Gen Y and everyone needing to understand how money and personal finance work. Twenty-something Ornella Grosz will help you recover, or better yet avoid, the slippery slope of debt!

Moneylicious: A Financial Clue for Generation Y explains the basis of investing, banking, purchasing a first home, the importance of spending with a touch of humor (yes, you can buy that $100 pair of jeans). And much more!

"For Gen Y . . . written by Gen Y . . . *Moneylicious* provides a great financial roadmap. Ornella's willingness to share her own stories not only engages the reader but creates a learning environment where the basics of money and investing are not only explained . . . but shared in a way that is entertaining as well as experiential. This book should be required reading for all young people in high school and college. Armed with the knowledge that Ornella shares, the readers will be prepared to not only survive . . . but to thrive in the financial world they face."

Sharon Lechter, Founder and CEO of Pay Your Family First,
member of the first President's Advisory Council
on Financial Literacy, the AICPA Financial Literacy
Commission and co-author of the National Bestseller
Think and Grow Rich—Three Feet From Gold

Friends of the Aspen Animal Shelter
a 501(c)(3) non-profit organization
www.dogsaspen.com

Friends of the Aspen Animal Shelter's mission primarily focuses on combating pet overpopulation and the consequences thereof. They offer a free spay/neuter/rescue campaign, which serves most of Colorado's Western Slope as well as the "Four Corners" region of Colorado, New Mexico, Utah, and Arizona. The exceptionally high volume of homeless pets located near Cortez and on the adjacent Indian Reservation Lands has resulted in one of Colorado's highest euthanasia rates. The non-profit's efforts reduce the number of animals euthanized in nearby shelters that have no alternative but to kill due to overcrowding.

How You Can Help Make Our Country a "No-Kill Nation"

- Adopt a shelter pet this year. Don't support pet shops where, more often than not, pets come from puppy and kitten mills.
- Spay/neuter your pets and support organizations that offer free or low-cost spay/neuter programs.
- Volunteer to foster pets from overcrowded shelters. You are saving a life by doing so.

Cover Katrina photo courtesy of
Nanette Martin

Shelter-Me Photography, Inc.
a 501(c)(3) non-profit organization
www.sheltermephotography.org

Nanette Martin is an international, award-winning editorial and documentary photographer and dedicated animal lover. After documenting the animal rescue effort in the wake of Hurricane Katrina, Nanette began photographing animals in the shelter system. She has photographed over 8,000 homeless animals, which has led to a significant increase in adoptions.

CPSIA information can be obtained at www.ICGtesting.com
Printed in the USA
LVOW051931070912

297645LV00002B/25/P

9 780985 273729